T0293506

FOUNDATIONS
OF
THE FUTURE
The Global Battle for Infrastructure

FOUNDATIONS
OF
THE FUTURE
The Global Battle for Infrastructure

Anthony H Rowley

NEW JERSEY · LONDON · SINGAPORE · BEIJING · SHANGHAI · HONG KONG · TAIPEI · CHENNAI · TOKYO

Published by

World Scientific Publishing Co. Pte. Ltd.

5 Toh Tuck Link, Singapore 596224

USA office: 27 Warren Street, Suite 401-402, Hackensack, NJ 07601

UK office: 57 Shelton Street, Covent Garden, London WC2H 9HE

Library of Congress Cataloging-in-Publication Data

Names: Rowley, Anthony, 1939–   author.

Title: Foundations of the future : the global battle for infrastructure / Anthony H Rowley.

Description: Singapore ; Hackensack, NJ : World Scientific Publishing Co. Pte. Ltd., [2020] |
    Includes index.

Identifiers: LCCN 2020004237 | ISBN 9789811218033 (hardcover) |
    ISBN 9789811218040 (ebook)

Subjects: LCSH: Infrastructure (Economics) | Yi dai yi lu (Initiative : China)

Classification: LCC HC79.C3 R69 2020 | DDC 338.9--dc23

LC record available at https://lccn.loc.gov/2020004237

Library Cataloguing-in-Publication Data

A catalogue record for this book is available from the British Library.

For any available supplementary material, please visit
https://www.worldscientific.com/worldscibooks/10.1142/11765#t=suppl

Desk Editor: Ong Shi Min Nicole

Typeset by Stallion Press
Email: enquiries@stallionpress.com

AUTHOR'S BIO

Anthony H. Rowley is a veteran journalist specialising in economic and financial affairs. He is a former Tokyo Correspondent of the *Singapore Business Times* and is now a regular columnist for the *South China Morning Post*. Prior to that, he held the positions of Business Editor and International Finance Editor at the *Far Eastern Economic Review*. He was Chief Editor of the World Bank's World Development Report on Infrastructure in 1994 and has also held the positions of Field Editor (Japan), Oxford Analytica and President of the Foreign Correspondents Club of Japan in Tokyo.

CONTENTS

INTRODUCTION

INFRASTRUCTURE: AN ECONOMIC AND STRATEGIC GAME CHANGER

It is difficult not to be awed by some of the infrastructural achievements of the past civilisations such as those of ancient Rome given those societies' lack of access to today's technologies. The long, straight highways and soaring viaducts and aqueducts built by the Roman Empire 2000 years ago to spread its military and commercial power across Europe are impressive examples. Yet, the world is on the verge again now of an infrastructure revolution that promises to transform our societies in terms of connectivity and communications. This too will involve awe-inspiring feats of construction that promise to be even more spectacular and extensive than anything seen in the past and to open up new vistas and prospects for economic prosperity and cultural fulfillment.

In the words of Amar Bhattacharya, a former senior World Bank official and now senior fellow of the Global Economy and Development Programme at the Brookings Institution in Washington, the next 20 years will be "more important for infrastructure development than at any time in history" (personal communication, October 2019). This is a bold statement but one that is likely to prove true if the infrastructure revolution that he and others envisage in coming decades does materialise. Basic infrastructure such as transport, communications, and energy systems will be required on an unprecedented scale to link advanced and emerging economies closer together — not just in the way that the telecommunications revolution has done but physically.

The COVID-19 pandemic will inevitably disrupt economic growth dramatically in 2020 and, to a lesser extent, beyond that, but it is unlikely to deflect the global economy from its medium to long-term growth path or to slow the universal demand for better physical infrastructure. If anything, the pandemic will heighten awareness of the need to prioritise socio-economic infrastructure provision in areas such as health care, sanitation, water and energy — adding to what was already a massive challenge even before the onset of the pandemic.

The coming decades will see "unique structural change (as Bhattacharya puts it) in the global economy and infrastructure will have a key role in this change. Strategic changes will radically shift the global balance of population and power. Over the next 20 years, the world will need to double its infrastructure stock involving total spending of 80 or 90 trillion dollars. Some 60–70 per cent of this colossal sum will be needed in emerging economies (led by China and India) to finance their transition from developing to advanced or even superpower status."

It promises to be money well spent because, as many experts assert, infrastructure is a key driver of economic growth. Jin Liqun, President and Chairman of the Asian Infrastructure Investment Bank (AIIB), for example, notes what he says is "clear evidence of a link between infrastructure investment and economic growth" (personal communication, 2017) while former Dean of the Asian Development Bank Institute, Naoyuki Yoshino expressed to the author his belief that "economic growth and investment in infrastructure go hand in hand" (personal communication, 2017) and likewise the G20 group of advanced and emerging economies has referred to infrastructure as a "key driver of economic growth and prosperity."

The vision articulated by such leading figures assumes that the onward march of globalisation will continue, requiring transport and communication networks to keep pace with this advance and making the world "smaller" in terms of connectivity. It is in many ways an inspiring vision, but it could be set back by growing nationalisms and the possible inability of many advanced and emerging nations to finance the multi-trillion-dollar investment required by the infrastructure revolution. Strategic considerations could also weigh more heavily than economic advantage in determining how far and how fast the infrastructure revolution is pursued. The impact that increased global connectivity is likely to have on an already stressed natural and social environment is another factor giving pause to the momentum for change and advance. And, there is no universal consensus on how the world can finance a major infrastructural refit.

Even so, infrastructure has moved to the centre stage in terms of global attention in recent years for a number of reasons. China's Belt and Road Initiative (BRI) has alerted the world to the potential for creating futuristic transport networks spreading across continents and seas and revolutionising the outlook for travel and commerce while digital and logistical advances also promise to shrink time and distance involved in communications.

Outside of China, the infrastructure debate is moving to centre stage for very different reasons. The approach of the US presidential election is likely to focus public attention sharply on infrastructural deficiencies there, which estimates suggest will require spending of around US$2 trillion beyond what is currently planned in order to repair and replace existing infrastructure. In its Infrastructure Report Card for 2017, the American Society of Civil Engineers awarded only a D-plus quality ranking to US infrastructure while noting that deteriorating roads, waterways, airports and seaports are having an adverse impact on growth, employment, productivity, public health and quality of life in the world's largest economy (cited in Little, 2020).

Bhattacharya sees the BRI as being "monumental on the scale of ambition" and he is not alone in this view (personal communication, 2019). It is shared, for example, by Director of the Reischauer Center for East Asian Studies at Johns Hopkins University, Kent Calder, who notes that the BRI "will develop infrastructure across a continent that historically has not been economically integrated, and which has conspicuously lacked infrastructure" (personal communication, 2017). The BRI is to the 21st century "what Rome was to Europe," Bhattacharya suggests (personal communication, 2019). "Rome was the imperial power and it built the connectivity of Europe in a way that has endured over millennia. In a similar way what China is aspiring to do is to build connectivity which recognizes that it is and going to be an economic power in the 21st century."

Observing Belt and Road projects such as the new Yongshun–Jishou Expressway in Hunan, Central China or the new 'Yaxi' Expressway running between Ya'an and Xichang in China's Sichuan province (see Fig. 0.1 (a) and Fig. 0.1 (b)), it is possible to share the view that China has taken over the mantle of ancient Rome as an infrastructure superpower. The project is spectacular — an inspiring feat of construction with highways and viaducts soaring vertiginously above valleys and gorges, snaking their way around mountains, and even interchanging at a kind of "spaghetti junction in the sky." The term infrastructure hardly seems adequate to describe the highway which, apart from being a marvel of

Figure 0.1 (a).   Spaghetti Junction in the Clouds — China's 'Yongji' Expressway.

Source: Depositphotos.com (2019). Copyright © Imaginechina-editorial / Depositphotos.com.

Figure 0.1 (b).   Expressway in the Clouds — China's 'Yaxi' Expressway.

Source: Xinhua.net. Retrieved 4 February 2020 from https://www.youtube.com/watch?v=xaKcw691qwy. Screenshot by author.

civil engineering, is arguably a symbol of what mankind's economic and social future could be like — one of global connectivity, human interchange, and commerce.

It is suggestive of a world where expressways and high-speed railways soar in a similar fashion over valleys and through mountains and across vast plains, making it possible to traverse continents in a fraction of the time it takes at present, yet without the deadening the sense of detachment that air travel creates. This would be a world in which the cultural and other joys of travel could be restored — with the option to rush on or linger at will. It would also be a world where goods flowed more speedily and in greater volumes around the world without the cost that air freight involves. Land and sea travel would join to make a richer reality of the term "globalisation."

Infrastructure, or at least transport infrastructure, is a key to such dreams — dreams that are capable of being transformed into reality using modern technology provided that the political will and financial wherewithal exist. Likewise, the huge benefits of energy and communications infrastructure are technically capable of being delivered universally. These may sound like flights of fancy to those accustomed to thinking of infrastructure as something much more mundane, but recreating the "romance" of infrastructure is a worthwhile ideal. Where they still exist, the viaducts and aqueducts of the former Roman Empire do still have the power to inspire admiration and awe, but that is because they are wonders of ancient civilisations. Modern civilisations are more impressed by contemplating the conquest of space which is seen as being more exciting than earthbound infrastructure. This applies equally to what excites the popular imagination and to what attracts capital investment.

But nations need literally to come down to earth in this regard. They need to pay more attention to the physical infrastructure upon which civilisation is built and to the decaying state that much of it is in nowadays especially in advanced economies. They need to imagine the possibilities that can be opened up for the future by increasing the physical connectivity between communities and countries and between markets and economies. Increased trade generates income and creates wealth, but it needs highways, railroads, and ports to support it. Connecting people via sophisticated wireless communications is well advanced in an age of Information and Artificial Intelligence, but this will be of limited use if peoples and markets are not better connected physically.

There is, of course, a "flip side" to the projected onward march of infrastructural connectivity across the world and that is its potential for damaging the environment if it is poorly designed — for example, by adding to rather than relieving congestion or by creating air and noise pollution. But turning back the clock on economic progress has never proved to be a viable solution to such problems. Effective design that protects the environment should surely be regarded as the preferred alternative.

This in turn raises the question of cost and that is something that does need to be confronted head on because quality does not come cheap. Japan has been a pioneer in promoting the concept of building "quality infrastructure" — a call which has been taken up by many advanced nations as a desirable aim. Setting aside the fact that the call is aimed partly at countering what Japan and others sometimes see as China's headlong dash to achieve global infrastructural connectivity at any cost (to the environment or to national budgets), the need for quality for quality infrastructure is very real.

Not only does the environment need to be protected against poor quality infrastructure but infrastructure itself — transport and energy networks in particular — needs to be protected against environmental change. Climate change threatens to wreak havoc on road, rail river, and power transmission systems through a dramatic rise in the incidence of flooding, hurricanes, rising sea levels, and other manifestations of natural or man-made damage. Proofing infrastructure against such risks (which are becoming clear and present dangers around the world) is possible, but costly.

In the Asia-Pacific region alone (according to the Asian Development Bank (2017)), the cost of insulating infrastructure from the perceived environmental risk will amount to nearly US$4 trillion in total between now and the year 2030. And this adds to a projected infrastructure building cost (even without such protections) of US$22.6 trillion during this period. It also increases the danger that there will be a yawning "gap" in infrastructure financing in advanced and developing countries alike between what public and private sectors of the global economy are currently providing and the projected needs for stepped-up spending (see Fig. 0.2). This issue is dealt with at some length in other chapters of this book.

How is this gap to be closed? A possible solution is in sight with the fast-growing awareness among investors of all types and sizes (in

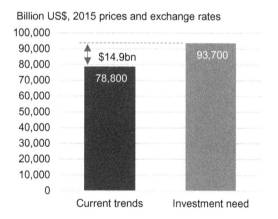

Figure 0.2.   The Infrastructure Gap.

Source: Oxford Economics (2017). Global Infrastructure Outlook. Oxford. Licensed from the Global Infrastructure Hub Ltd under a Creative Commons Attribution 3.0 Australia License.

parts of Europe especially but increasingly in America and Asia) of the need for private savings to be directed in much greater amounts in future into what is becoming known as "sustainable investment." In particular, these funds need to be directed into what are known as the Sustainable Development Goals or SDGs announced in 2015 by the United Nations. Among the 17 principal goals identified as necessary in order to sustain economic and social development and to reduce poverty to more acceptable levels by 2030, only one applies directly to infrastructure but various other goals are linked indirectly to the same end (United Nations, 2015).

According to the UN (2019), private sector contributions of around US\$2 trillion annually will be required to supplement public sector funds in order to achieve these goals (well in excess of what is currently being provided). Sums of this magnitude are available in theory from private savings and investments (which total an estimated US\$270 trillion on a global basis), but the conduits for channelling such sums into infrastructure and other SDGs do not yet exist in a form that is easily identifiable to investors. There are other conduits available such as the so-called environmental, social, and governance (ESG) investing, which encourages the corporate sector to invest in such socially and economically desirable areas. But the amount of investment which such generalised targets can actually direct toward infrastructure as an asset class is uncertain and may prove inadequate to meet projected needs.

This book deals principally with the issue of transport, energy, and communications infrastructure in Asia, the world's most populous region which for all its economic progress still has huge areas of poverty and uneven development. Asia is also the region where infrastructure demands will be among the biggest in the world if the region is to continue growing economically while also protecting its environment. What applies to Asia will apply increasingly to Africa in the future, while the infrastructure needs of Latin America and other regions are also huge.

The need to boost infrastructure investment is not limited to the developing world, however. The world's largest economy, that of the United States, is in urgent need of at least US$1 trillion investment for new or replacement infrastructure if it is to maintain its "advanced" status. US President Donald Trump tacitly acknowledged this reality in mid 2020 when he revived his ambition to devote US$1 trillion to upgrading the basic infrastructure of the world's largest economy. Much of the basic infrastructure in the US is decaying and in some cases is in a dangerous state of disrepair. This threatens public health and safety in everything from highways and railways to drains and sewers. Critically, delays in business transactions caused by inadequate infrastructure result in the estimated loss of hundreds of millions of dollars a year in the US alone. Much the same applies to parts of Europe and beyond.

There are, it is true, few parts of the world that cannot be reached nowadays by land or by sea, but it is often at considerable cost in terms of money and time. If the world were served universally by superhighways and high-speed rail systems along with modern maritime facilities, goods could flow much more rapidly and easily, leading to lower costs, creating new demand, and boosting production and employment. Production "supply chains" in manufacturing could operate more efficiently and (importantly) bring many more developing nations into the supply network. All this is to say nothing of the benefits of enhanced human and cultural interchange.

Yet, instead of focussing on how to expand global connectivity and commercial exchange, there is a danger that the world could again become enveloped by trade protectionism and trade wars — by a fortress mentality rather than by "outreach." Legislating for free trade and open markets, though such reform is essential, will not of itself produce a more prosperous global economy and bring about improvements in social welfare. The world urgently needs to strengthen and expand the infrastructural foundations upon which trade and commerce are built, literally as well as figuratively. Instead, the world risks sliding not only into trade wars but also into infrastructure wars.

For all its status as a wonder of modern civil engineering and technology, the Chengdu–Lhasa Highway is also a symbol of this danger — of the dichotomy between the unifying and, yet at the same time, divisive potential of physical connectivity. The highway is part of the ambitious BRI, which is designed to link China's massive land mass with that of Western Europe, via Central Asia, and with Africa via the Middle East using both land and sea routes — a "belt" of transcontinental highways and maritime "roads." The potential of this grand endeavour to link peoples and countries physically is clear; less obvious is the danger of creating suspicion and confrontation. In a truly globalised world, a hemisphere-girdling venture like the Belt and Road would be undertaken by an international consortium acting within a global consensus. But China has decided to go it alone precisely because there is no such consensus. The United States, Japan, and Australia have since launched competitive undertakings in the shape of the so-called Trilateral Partnership while India too is considering rival schemes. All this points to a global malaise in attitudes toward infrastructure.

China has been one of the few leading nations to see infrastructure as a means to an end and has been prepared to marshal huge resources into achieving that end, an example which is now being emulated elsewhere because of the perceived China threat. For all the many attacks on China's alleged motives in creating the BRI, there is no denying the "vision" behind it and it is a vision that appears to work. As head of the AIIB, Jin Liqun (personal communication, 2017) notes, "There is empirical evidence showing an undeniable link between infrastructure investment and economic growth." And as Jin observes, it was "largely owing to the broad benefits of improved infrastructure that China has managed to lift over 500 million people out of poverty (by World Bank standards) in a little over two decades. The percentage of [China's] population living in poverty fell from 65 per cent in 1981 to just 4 per cent" during this time.

China's vision is not just about creating domestic growth. It flows from a belief that the sum of the parts beyond China's borders can add up to something greater than the present whole. The parts in this case are scores of countries that stretch thousands of miles along the route of the BRI. The world has scarcely begun to exploit the economic potential yet of these countries in terms of the vast natural and human resources to be found in places like Northeast Asia, Africa, Latin America, and others. It is one thing, however, to have such a vision and another to implement it. This is basically why China's President Xi Jinping launched the BRI and coupled it with what Kent Calder terms the "brilliant" idea of creating an AIIB to help finance the grand design.

This dual initiative took the world's leading economies off guard. They reacted defensively and even aggressively in some cases. The BRI, along with the AIIB, has been criticised as an alleged example of Chinese economic and strategic neo-imperialism, as a form of "debt-trap diplomacy" and (at a rather more mundane level) as a covert means for China to export its surplus construction and production capacity. Even if there are elements of truth in some of these charges, they often smack of resentment at the fact that China has sought to assume the role of global leader on infrastructure.

They also point to frustration on the part of many advanced nations at the fact that they appear unable to "get their act together" when it comes to infrastructure provision. Policymakers in Western nations are often conflicted when it comes to the question of whether or not they should pursue infrastructure initiatives. Social welfare considerations and the desire to please electorates by supplying them with new infrastructure may argue in favour of a proactive approach. But the fear of being accused of failure to put projects to the "market test" — i.e. whether there is proven demand for a facility and proof that it can pay for itself — argues for caution. Business firms that need to justify investments to their shareholders (often on a short-term basis) also lean toward caution. Social pressure groups meanwhile demand that governments account for their infrastructure actions in detail and at great length.

Institutional investors such as pension funds, life assurance companies, sovereign wealth funds, and others have the financial wherewithal (scores of trillions of dollars in total) to play a much larger role in infrastructure financing than they do at present. But financial (although not "economic") returns on infrastructure investment cannot easily compete with those on manufacturing and services in the short term, and that deters investment in infrastructure. Even multilateral development banks (such as the World Bank and regional banks) that were purpose-built to finance infrastructure are constrained by political limitations in addressing infrastructure. How to resolve these problems is by no means simple and straightforward. It will require changes in the way savings are collected and in priorities for investing them. It is also likely to require a fundamental rebalancing of how public and private sector resources are deployed.

All this helps to explain why nations that pioneered both industrial and infrastructural revolutions a century or more ago and also underwent infrastructural revival in the decades following World War II should be languishing now in a state of infrastructural decline and decay. Their transport and energy infrastructure are inferior in some cases to that of emerging economies that launched their industrial revolutions much more recently, especially those that were part of the so-called "East Asian Economic Miracle."

Foremost among these latter economies is China, whose infrastructural development since the nation's economy began to open up to the outside world and modernise from the early 1980s has been little short of stunning. The degree of overall economic development in China has also been very impressive and, as Jin Liqun says, infrastructure has played a great part in both. The Chinese model "works" so far as infrastructure is concerned but the combination of state ownership and central command of the economy which has made this possible is unlikely to appeal to many Western economies.

In market economies, the critical question of how to direct the huge savings that are invested through private financial institutions into infrastructure (so as to supplement tax revenues and user charges) needs to be addressed as a matter of urgency. Resolving this problem will require bold decisions on the part of policymakers. Some suggestions for reform are offered in the concluding chapter of this book. They range from introducing special infrastructure taxes and issuing more infrastructure bonds to greater use of public provident funds in order to finance infrastructure. One suggested approach involving the collection of "spillover" taxes generated by business development along the routes of highways and railways and channelling these to infrastructure investors is also examined.

Following this Introduction, this book suggests in Chapter 1 that the world is in the midst of an "infrastructure war" which Western nations risk losing as China's BRI marches boldly across the Eurasian continent, bringing economic and strategic advantage to China and to countries along its route, while other major powers struggle to keep pace. China is in a sense "weaponising" infrastructure by creating a nexus of road, rail, and sea connections spanning half the world to secure prosperity-enhancing trade and investment opportunities and to project both hard (economic) and soft (cultural) power in the process. The inability of Western nations to respond fully up to now reflects their failure on the one hand to appreciate the importance of transport, energy, and communications infrastructure in generating economic activity and, on the other hand, the strong bias toward short-termism in the approach of market economies toward capital investment.

Chapter 2 looks at where in the world infrastructure needs are greatest (in emerging and advanced economies) with a special focus upon Asia where spending is expected to be the highest in the world in coming decades if the region is to maintain past high levels of economic growth on the one hand and on the other hand to cope with a continuing burden of reducing poverty. Chapter 3 then examines why Western advanced economies are falling behind in the "race" to modernise infrastructure and the factors that are constraining their progress in this regard.

Chapter 4 looks more closely at the BRI and what it hopes to achieve; at the geographical scope of the project and its possible financial cost. The supporting role played by the China-led AIIB is also reviewed in this chapter. Chapter 5 then examines rival schemes to the BRI, principally the Asia–Africa Growth Corridor (AAGC) promoted jointly by Japan and India and the Trilateral Partnership among the United States, Japan, and Australia. Chapter 6 suggests that the East–West struggle for economic and strategic position and advantage in infrastructure has elements of the "Great Game" fought among rival powers in the 19th century, but this time with higher stakes.

Chapter 7 examines the key issue of who will pay the huge bill for global infrastructure provision as between state and private sector players, while Chapter 8 looks at some proposed novel solutions to the problem of how to meet infrastructure investment needs. Chapter 9 casts light on the "dark side" of infrastructure financing — corruption in contract awards and implementation, while Chapter 10 then puts infrastructure into the broad context of sustainable investment. Chapter 11 looks at the important and topical issue of quality versus quantity in infrastructure planning and outlays, while Chapter 12 examines the critical role of multilateral development banks (MDBs) in infrastructure financing and operation. It suggests that the role played by these invaluable institutions is subject in many cases to political and ideological constraints that severely limit their usefulness as providers of infrastructure. Conclusions are drawn following Chapter 12.

CHAPTER 1

INFRASTRUCTURE AND THE RISE AND FALL OF NATIONS

We are in the midst of a global infrastructure war. The conflict has not made headlines, and most people are even unaware that it is happening. Yet the outcome of this battle will go far to determine which nations emerge as winners and which nations turn out to be losers in the battle for strategic and economic supremacy in the future. Unless Western societies wake up to the reality of the infrastructure war — and the fact that they are in danger of losing it — victory will likely go to the emerging nations led by China, where infrastructure is a national priority, and not to developed nations like the United States and Europe, where infrastructure has been given lower priority in recent decades.

Relatively few people have regarded infrastructure as a key factor behind China's rapid ascent to second place behind the United States in the league table of global economies, with the likelihood that it could become number one by around 2030 in terms of total output. Likewise, few have viewed infrastructural decay as a major factor behind the decline of economic vigour in "advanced" nations, especially in the case of the United States and Europe. Other explanations are often advanced such as ageing populations, lower levels of investment and productivity, the continuing legacy of the Global Financial Crisis, or historical inevitability as economies "mature."

Yet there is ample evidence that the state of a nation's basic infrastructure — transport, energy, and communications networks in particular — is a significant factor influencing the economic growth. China for one has enjoyed very high growth rates for four consecutive decades while growth has lagged in advanced economies, where ageing and decaying infrastructure creates transport bottlenecks and other economic inefficiencies (not to mention physical danger and social inconvenience).

What might be termed the "romance" of infrastructure and its ability to link people and nations, to enhance social welfare and to boost economic growth seems to be lost now on half of the world — the more developed half. Infrastructure projects there are often dismissed as being "white elephants" or "bridges to nowhere" while maintenance and repair are also neglected. The dramatic collapse of a major highway bridge in Italy in 2018 and a similar collapse in Minnesota, USA, 10 years earlier, both causing multiple fatalities and injuries, was literally shocking evidence of this neglect. These and similar incidents in Japan and elsewhere sent a strong signal that infrastructure in many developed economies is outdated and decaying.

It may seem far-fetched to suggest that infrastructure determines the economic fate of nations, and yet history provides some interesting examples in this regard. China's famous Silk Road served as a conduit for international commerce for more than 1,500 years while ancient Rome built highways, bridges, viaducts, and other civil engineering marvels that served as arteries of international commerce and imperial rule (see Fig. 1.1). In more recent times, Britain's industrial revolution relied upon a revolution in canal, rail, and road infrastructure. America came to birth on the back of vast transport networks that brought the east and west of the continent

Figure 1.1. When in Rome. Roman Aqueduct at Pont du Gard France near Nimes. Its lower tier carries a road over the river, whereas the upper tiers contain an aqueduct that carried water to Nimes, ca 1st century A.D.
Source: Photograph used under license from Benh Lieu Song under a Creative Commons 3.0 License.

together, as was likewise the case in Canada while Japan underwent similar experiences following the Meiji Revolution of 1868.

Western nations have since lost their vision with regard to infrastructure. We live in an age of "globalisation", and yet the attitude of advanced nations has become parochial when it comes to physical connectivity between countries and continents. There are few grand initiatives in transport linkages of the kind that triggered quantum leaps in trade and productivity in the past. Motor vehicle and marine vessel technologies have advanced greatly, but development of a Pan-European or Pan-American network of highways, railways, and ports has not kept pace.

The story is different in Asia where, as subsequent chapters of this book make clear, bold new initiatives are being taken in terrestrial and marine transport infrastructure (see Fig. 1.2). This Asian infrastructure "assault" is vitally necessary in what has become the world's fastest growing and most populous region — and it is a tribute to Asian pragmatism that infrastructure is receiving such official attention at a time when spending is languishing elsewhere. Expert estimates suggest

Billion US$, 2015 prices and exchange rates

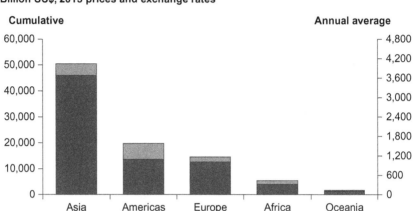

Figure 1.2.   The Infrastructure Gap.

Source: Oxford Economics (2017). Global Infrastructure Outlook, Oxford. Licensed from the Global Infrastructure Hub Ltd under a Creative Commons Attribution 3.0 Australia License.

that between US$70 and US$100 trillion of spending on new basic infrastructure will be required globally by the year 2030 and the Asian Development Bank has suggested that one-quarter to one-third of this (US$26 trillion) will need to be spent in the Asia-Pacific region alone. The bulk of this investment will need to be in power generation followed by transport and telecommunications (see Fig. 1.3).

Infrastructure may appear rather mundane alongside technological marvels such as Artificial Intelligence or space travel. It is not a star performer either when it comes to capturing the popular imagination. Infrastructure is all too often taken for granted as something that is "there" to serve us, whether in the form of highways to drive on, trains to ride in, or electrical energy or systems to serve our insatiable appetite for Internet communications. Few people pay much attention to the question of who provides such services — just as long as they do not become too expensive. Myriad consumer goods and services have first claim on people's attention and on their purses.

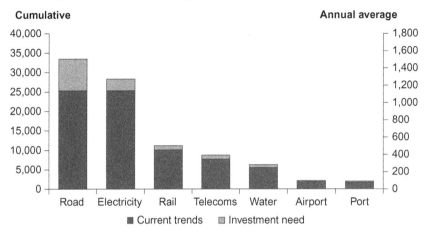

Billion US$, 2015 prices and exchange rates

Figure 1.3.   Which Sectors are Neediest?

Source: Oxford Economics (2017). Global Infrastructure Outlook, Oxford. Licensed from the Global Infrastructure Hub Ltd under a Creative Commons Attribution 3.0 Australia License.

Yet the modern world relies critically upon "connectivity" between countries, communities, and markets. Whoever controls these connections controls much of the world. This is true irrespective of whether we are talking of terrestrial highways, sea lanes, or energy and communications networks. There is a strong strategic element to infrastructure because control or ownership of land and sea facilities (such as, for example, the control and ownership that China is coming to enjoy under its Belt and Road Initiative (BRI)) implies access to key trading and supply arteries, which has military as well as economic implications.

Consider also the fact that global manufacturing is now fed by myriad production "supply chains" that bind together the world's major and minor economies. These are of key importance from an economic point of view. China's trans-Eurasia BRI is designed partly to link the country's industrial heartland, which is moving increasingly to the Western part of China, to key industrial areas in Europe which are migrating increasingly to the eastern part of the Continent.

Setting aside the strategic implications of transport linkages, manufacturing supply chains are of key importance to business and a slow pace in providing cross-border transport infrastructure means that markets for goods produced by these supply networks are of less than optimum "scale."

The size of the infrastructure challenge has grown dramatically as former developing nations have emerged as leading players on the world economic stage and as the need has grown to connect them not only with international consumer markets but also with one another. At the same time, the rapid growth of major cities, towns, and other urban agglomerations around the world is placing a huge strain on infrastructure. Into the bargain, the need to make infrastructure proof against the ravages of climate change and natural disasters is significantly inflating an already huge infrastructure spending bill.

The term "connectivity" is often used in the context of the Information Technology or IT revolution, which has in a sense "brought together" hundreds of millions of people within countries and continents through the medium of Internet platforms. But global connectivity has not begun to keep pace when it comes to linking people and businesses physically. Google, Facebook, Alibaba, and others deliver billions of bytes of information from IT platforms, but Amazon and its "e-commerce" equivalents cannot deliver goods without the aid of physical infrastructure. The Internet age has seen IT companies become the darlings of stock markets, able to raise billions of dollars of finance without difficulty. Yet construction and engineering enterprises involved in infrastructure building struggle to raise a fraction of these amounts, as do governments.

Nor is development of the full potential of IT unconnected to the need for infrastructure development. As an example, China's proposed Digital Silk Road that would provide advanced communications infrastructure primarily for data transmission and IT use on the 5G standard to countries along the Belt and Road, including undersea cable, transmission and other facilities, has since become an increasingly important, part of the BRI.

Government-funded infrastructure projects are often viewed nowadays in advanced Western economies as being alien to market principles, while no viable alternative to state-led initiatives has emerged. Private-sector initiatives have fallen well short of expectations that prevailed a decade or two ago. Many policymakers in Western nations seem to be unaware of the dangers they are courting and the benefits they are foregoing by neglecting infrastructure. As the Asian Development Bank Institute in Tokyo has noted, infrastructure remains a "greatly under-researched" subject (Yoshino, Helble, & Abidhadjaev, 2018; World Economic Forum, 2015a). Yet studies that have been carried out so far strongly support the view that it is very closely linked to economic growth and human welfare.

As observed in the Introduction, Jin Liqun, president and chairman of the China-led Asian Infrastructure Investment Bank (AIIB), makes a simple but profound point when he says there is clear "evidence of a link between infrastructure investment and economic growth" (personal communication, 2017). China's views are shared increasingly in East Asia and beyond as the country's influence radiates outwards. The World Bank has acknowledged that China has been "the fastest growing country in the world for the past few decades" and that "one of the defining features has been investment-led growth underpinned by massive development of physical infrastructure." China's experience, the World Bank says, suggests that other countries should "design an economic policy that improves infrastructure as well as human capital formation."

Many economists agree that investment in transport, energy, and communications infrastructure can have a strong "multiplier effect" by creating much more value than the size of the financial investment involved. Good infrastructure reduces business costs, generates employment and increases the size of a nation's tax base. The World Economic Forum states that there is a "positive correlation" between infrastructure investment and the growth of a country's gross domestic product or GDP" (see Fig. 1.4; World Economic Forum, 2015b). The Asian Development Bank Institute too states that "economic growth and investment in infrastructure go hand in hand" (Yoshino, Helble, & Abidhadjaev, 2018), while the G20 group of advanced and emerging economies refer to infrastructure as a "key driver of economic growth and prosperity."

Infrastructure is no longer just a matter of "steel and concrete" construction. Myriad resources and skills are needed in its design, construction, and operation in an age where Information Technology and Artificial Intelligence play a key role alongside civil engineering. As commerce becomes increasingly IT-driven, the need for sophisticated "multi-modal" transport systems is rising in line with the demand for high-speed delivery of goods and services.

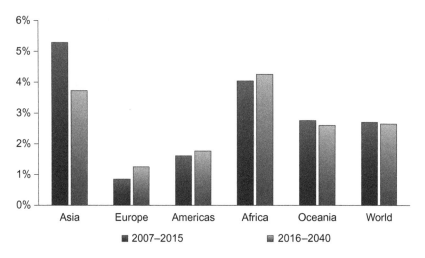

Figure 1.4.   How Grows the World.

Source: Oxford Economics (2017). Global Infrastructure Outlook, Oxford. Licensed from the Global Infrastructure Hub Ltd under a Creative Commons Attribution 3.0 Australia License.

Infrastructure has in fact become a "growth industry" in itself, one that drives technological innovation, spurs productivity, and generates new types of demand and employment.

Yet in the same way that infrastructure investment can bring real gains in the economic and social welfare of nations, neglect can entail major financial and other losses. For example, the American Society of Civil Engineers (ASCE) states that the US economy could lose nearly US$4 trillion in GDP between 2016 and 2025 if infrastructure investment gaps are not filled properly. This could reach US$14 trillion by 2040 if the nation's ageing roads, railways, and bridges are left to decay. The ASCE estimates that losses to business sales will reach US$7 trillion by 2025, while by 2040, it could reach US$23 trillion.

Inadequate infrastructure will also have an adverse effect on disposable household income. Between 2016 and 2025, each American household will lose US$3,400 every year due to infrastructure deficiencies, the ASCE estimates. The economic impact will also cost some 2.5 million jobs by 2020. Without more new infrastructure investment, Americans can look forward to increased traffic jams, airport bottlenecks, and power outages. Deterioration of port, road, train, water, and electric facilities will also take an economic toll in the form of lost sales and higher costs.

In a survey by the World Economic Forum in 2017, the US was placed only in the 15th position for railroad infrastructure and 14th for quality of roads. The UK meanwhile ranked well down the list at the 30th position. Switzerland heads some infrastructure polls, having maximised its advantage as a nexus of European connectivity by building world-class infrastructure. The Netherlands, Finland, France, and Austria also rank among the top half dozen states in terms of infrastructure quality. Even so, the European Investment Bank has warned that Europe in general is "risking its future prosperity by spending too little on infrastructure." Other research sources place Hong Kong and Singapore as co-equal at the top in terms of infrastructure endowments. Both have invested in infrastructure to leverage their positions as trade entrepôts. Japan too ranks among the world's top-half dozen countries in terms of its infrastructure, while South Korea, Taiwan, and Malaysia are also highly placed.

Unlike advanced Western nations, China (still a "developing" economy by World Trade Organization definitions) has equipped itself with some of the world's most advanced infrastructure and has in a sense "weaponized" infrastructure by launching its BRI to connect the nation's vast landmass and economy with those of Europe (via Central Asia) and also with the Middle East and Africa by means of land and maritime networks. These transport arteries are designed to revive former "Silk Road" trade routes through which Imperial China conducted international commerce centuries or even millennia ago.

The name of the game in infrastructure now is not simply connectivity, however. It has elements of the "Great Game" played out in the 19th century in Central Asia by rival European powers seeking strategic advantage — only this time it is being played out on a much grander scale. In this connection, China's BRI is proving to be as controversial as it is bold and has provoked competitive responses from the US, Japan, India, Australia, and others, which have proposed building their own infrastructure networks in and beyond Asia. Japan and India have jointly proposed an Asia–Africa Growth Corridor (AAGC), which in some aspects resembled China's BRI.

Washington has proposed a US-led Trilateral Partnership, comprising of the US, Japan, and Australia, and embracing infrastructure development and other forms of economic cooperation. This partnership emphasizes the need to promote private-sector development rather than the Chinese model of state enterprise-driven development.

The European Commission too has drawn up a plan entitled "The European Way to Connectivity" for managing the task of connecting Europe with Asia.

The wider significance of these moves is often overlooked, but they point to a threat of infrastructure wars in the future. If infrastructure can be weaponised as a way of achieving strategic advantage, the winners of the ensuing battles will be those nations that are best able to channel financial and other resources into the infrastructure needed to project economic and perhaps military power. This is where the vulnerability of the US and some European economies is being exposed. Unlike China, theirs are not "command" economies, and economic agents cannot simply be ordered to direct financial and other resources into infrastructure.

The sheer scale of China's Belt and Road plan matches the speed with which the world's second largest economy has equipped itself with domestic high-speed rail networks, superhighways, and other transport and communications arteries. China's initiative has underlined the ability of state economies to marshal resources into infrastructure at a speed and on a scale that market economies find it difficult to match. China is investing heavily in African infrastructure where the potential to tap future markets and natural resources is vast. It is also active in building infrastructure in Latin America. South Korea too is planning to link its road and rail systems with those of North Korea and from there on into China.

Why has the West been underinvesting in infrastructure? There are multiple reasons, but put simply, neo-liberal economic models that have prevailed for the past 30 years or so in Western nations have rendered public spending on infrastructure politically difficult. Neo-liberal orthodoxy holds that government spending is at best inefficient and at worst damaging or subject to corruption and that only private investment motivated by profit and guided by market forces can efficiently allocate resources. Yet despite evidence (including the Global Financial Crisis and the Great Recession a decade ago) that the neo-liberal economic paradigm does not work, lack of persuasive alternative models has hindered the progress of other approaches.

China's BRI was born into this intellectual and policy vacuum, and it has awakened some of the world's leading market economies to the shortcomings of their systems when it comes to mobilising the sums needed for infrastructure. As noted, the United States, Japan, and Australia as well as India have united their efforts under the banner of the "Trilateral Partnership" which was launched at the end of 2018 to counter China's Belt and Road project. They are making infrastructure in the Indo-Pacific regions a "top priority, from roads to railways, ports to pipelines, airports and data-lines." This competition is taking place in what are ostensibly two different theatres — the "Asia-Pacific" region which China is coming to dominate and the so-called "Indo-Pacific" region centring on the Indian Ocean. In reality, the two areas overlap, and this threatens to become a source of friction.

China's own domestic infrastructural foundations are now in a highly advanced stage nationally in terms of intercity and interregional connectivity even if urban infrastructure outside of major town and cities is not so well developed. Since 1980, when the country's modernisation began to get underway six-lane highways and high-speed rail systems have criss-crossed its vast terrain, spreading economic and social development from the eastern coastal regions to the landlocked western part of the country and on into Central Asia and beyond. But it is not just the high and sustained rates of economic growth China has achieved that render what is happening there significant for the rest of the world. Economic revival is part of a long-term strategy to project power and influence into all corners of the Earth. China has launched a kind of infrastructure blitzkrieg within which the projection of economic and strategic power via "hard" infrastructure is accompanied by a "soft power" assault in creating new institutions that serve to support China's global vision.

One key element of this strategy has been the launching of the AIIB to work alongside the BRI. The AIIB is designed with broad objectives in mind. These are to challenge the post-war economic order in which the United States has dominated multilateral development institutions. The AIIB is aimed at providing China with a "voice" with which to address global economic issues, and to do so in concert with a large contingent of other developing and advanced nations that are among its now 130 shareholders (led by China, India, and Russia) from developing and advanced nations alike. The AIIB itself promises to become part of a new developing "infrastructure" of global governance and finance.

Other major powers have reacted with criticism. They have alleged lack of transparency and non-representation of participating countries in decision making in the case of both the BRI and the AIIB. China has been accused of lending huge sums of money to infrastructure projects that burden host countries with debt — deliberately creating a "debt trap" and allowing Beijing to seize control of strategically important infrastructure as loan collateral. Rather than being a matter of "debt trap diplomacy" on China's part, this reflects according to people such as Hiroshi Watanabe, former head of the Japan Bank for International Cooperation (a major global infrastructure lender), a lack of adequate due diligence of BRI projects by an institutionally immature AIIB and by other Chinese state-lending institutions which have been over-zealous in their credit allocation.

If Western nations are to compete successfully with China in terms of infrastructure provision at home and overseas, what is required is not a more widespread adoption of a socialist model so much as a form of "capitalism with socialist characteristics." The public sector needs to assume a wider role in helping unleash the resources of the private sector. Governments need to articulate a vision of infrastructure development and channel resources into realising that vision; they need to act as underwriters or "lenders of last resort" for infrastructure projects so that the private sector can become more heavily involved.

Governments have a unique ability to underwrite risk, given their access to tax revenues and their ability to issue bonds, which find ready buyers among central banks and financial institutions. By using their access to resources and acting as guarantors on a much larger scale than is the case at present, governments have the power to unleash a torrent of private-sector finance across a wide swathe of infrastructure activity. Relatively few of the risks they underwrite are likely to crystallise as official liabilities, but what matters is the presence of the guarantor.

Savings held in western financial institutions are estimated by the International Finance Corporation (an arm of the World Bank) at around US$270 trillion, of which only a fraction currently find their way into infrastructure. Governments finance some 70 per cent of infrastructure investment in emerging and developing economies while private-sector investment amounts to only 20 per cent. The rest comes from multilateral development institutions such as the World Bank. In advanced economies too, governments are the biggest spenders. Yet, while governments are expected to shoulder the major part of the burden of financing infrastructure, they face the risk of a taxpayer revolt or a government bond market crisis if they commit too much money directly to the sector. By using their powers to guarantee borrowing, however, they can leverage infrastructure lending hugely.

A good analogy is with multilateral development banks such as the World Bank. Governments that own these institutions provide their capital but only a fraction of it has actually to be "paid in". The rest is "callable" only in an emergency, and yet by simply pledging to pay in capital, governments enable the development banks to leverage up massively in international debt markets. Even so, many of these purpose-built development banks are greatly underused in infrastructure. Instead, they are charged with myriad tasks ranging from medical and social welfare responsibilities to gender issues, money laundering, and even drug control. Partly as a result of such deficiencies and the misallocation of resources, infrastructure investment in advanced countries has sunk to historically low levels, declining from over 6 per cent of gross domestic product in the late 1960s to less than 4 per cent now (McKinsey Global Institute, 2016). By contrast, in emerging and developing nations (such as those in Asia especially), infrastructure investment has been running at double this level — averaging 8 per cent of GDP since 2008.

China's emergence as a major global player in infrastructure is triggering more debate on the relative roles of the state versus the private sector in providing for the needs of this key sector. Western nations need to tackle shortcomings in their own systems more vigorously, especially those relating to the collection of savings and the need to channel more of these into infrastructure. Reaction to the "China challenge" in infrastructure has been defensive so far rather than provoking acknowledgement that there is a problem of resource allocation within market economies when it comes to infrastructure.

Infrastructure development has been central to shifts in the structure of the global economy and in the balance of power in recent decades, which is one reason why some advanced nations have reacted defensively to the prospect that China's BRI presents an acceleration in this process. As Amar Bhattacharya, a former senior World Bank official, notes, a critical change that has been underway for some time is a shift of the economic fulcrum from advanced economies to emerging markets and developing countries. "China was part of the first wave but what we are seeing now is a much broader transformation encompassing other parts of Asia and Africa," he says. Among the population of the world, some six out of seven live in the developing world, and as their incomes rise, their demands for infrastructure services will rise. Another critical change, he observes, is urbanisation. As of now, roughly one half of the world's population of seven billion live in urban centres. By 2050, the world population will reach 9 billion, of which 70 per cent are expected to live in urban areas. "There will be more people moving to urban settlements in these next two or three decades than at any time in history and urbanisation is a huge force for infrastructure development."

The shift from agriculture and rural living to manufacturing and services activity in urban areas implies that urban land area will double in the next 20 years and that urban population will double in the next 35 years. In line with these changes and the shift towards more infrastructure-intensive living, the stock of infrastructure is expected to double in the next 15–20 years. At the same time, climate change will demand more climate-resilient infrastructure.

Much of the infrastructure that has been built in the past is not "fit for purpose" argues Bhattacharya, who was formerly Director of The Group of 24 developing country finance ministers and central bank governors. "It is engineered almost to promote congestion. If you plunk down a road without forward thinking, then it will breed congestion. It will not solve the problem. You have to take the long view and think in a spatial [context] to produce compactness rather than causing sprawl and crawl."

The United Nations Intergovernmental Panel on Climate Change (IPCC) has suggested that the world has 12 years in which to get infrastructure right. "If we want to meet these structural transformations or growth objectives, we have to update our infrastructure," observes Bhattacharya. And it needs to be designed in such a way so as to cut carbon emissions by at least 35 per cent. "There is tremendous urgency to actually getting our act together. That is why it is so important to look at systems — energy systems, transport systems, cities, etcetera — and at whether are they fit for purpose and also to look at countries' investment and growth trajectories and ask whether those are fit for purpose."

Infrastructure is the leading driver in shaping other (forms of) capital. It shapes the physical capital because every type of production develops around it. If done well, it forms social capital and rebuilds and preserves natural capital. And so, in that sense, rethinking infrastructure today to think about what kind of growth we want for the 21st century is what I have in mind. Today the stock of infrastructure or of capital in the world does not match these requirements.

"It is not economically efficient; it produces a lot of negative externalities of which carbon is only one; it produces congestion and pollution and it is destroying natural habitats and ecosystems. That capital stock is not really what is needed, and yet there is the possibility for a much better stock. Experience in Britain, Hong Kong, Japan or China, shows that it is possible to have infrastructure which is much more economically efficient and that can produce much better outcomes in terms of compact cities, sustainable mobilities, vibrant communities, resilient and robust and fruitful ecosystems; All these things are actually possible with the technology that we have today."

In order to achieve the needed transformation, it will be necessary to accelerate the replacement of ageing and polluting technologies and capital stock such as coal-fired power plants and congested road, not only in advanced economies but also in China and India, Bhattacharya argues. The second challenge will be to ensure that all new infrastructure is built to as high a standard as possible. This, stresses Bhattacharya, "is not only about producing good social and economic outcomes; it is also crucial for the survival of the Earth. We do have the technological possibility, and the knowledge policy to get things right. So, keeping pressure on will be of tremendous importance."

CHAPTER 2

WHERE IN THE WORLD ARE INFRASTRUCTURE NEEDS GREATEST?

The world — and that means advanced and emerging economies alike — needs a huge amount of new infrastructure in everything from transportation linkages, energy systems, and communication networks to basic water supply and drainage if the global economy is to keep moving forward and if social needs are to be provided for. The trouble is that no one seems to know exactly how much infrastructure is needed, where the needs are greatest, and how much it will cost. Moreover, no one is sure about how and by whom the needed infrastructure is going to be paid for. This is a remarkable situation in an age when advanced nations pride themselves on the volumes of "big data" they are able to marshal and their ability to process it at lightning speed.

Mapping the need for infrastructure spending on a global basis is an essential and overdue task. What has prevented this from being done has to do partly with an ideological bias against public sector initiatives. Arguably, too much faith has been reposed in the ability of the private sector to supply and manage infrastructure even though governments (which are still responsible for provisioning most of the infrastructure worldwide) are in a better position to assess the needs than the private sector, made up as it is of myriad players in multiple nations. Partly because official inputs have not been sought on a sufficient scale, much of the world finds itself now in a state of relative ignorance about the state of infrastructure.

The explosion of economic growth in developing and emerging economies that occurred from the 1980s onwards ought to have alerted policymakers to the fact that huge strains would be imposed on the world's infrastructural underpinnings, in terms of transport, energy, and communications, especially. An understanding of what this implied for infrastructure needs at the national and international levels is essential if economic growth and development along with social welfare are not to suffer. The requirement needs to be properly mapped and quantified in countries around the world.

Instead, the potential deficit in infrastructure that is needed to underpin the process of globalisation has gone largely unrecognised by governments (those of Western nations, especially) as well as by multilateral institutions and financial markets. When the author of this book was engaged in 1994 to act as the chief external editor of the World Bank's World Development Report on infrastructure and inquired as to whether the document would include an inventory of global needs and an assessment of the possible contributions from public and private sectors, he was politely informed that it was "possible to move the furniture but not the walls" of the report.

What this rather cryptic comment meant was that development ideology as enshrined in the then prevailing "Washington Consensus" did not allow of any admission that the private sector might not be able to assume the task of infrastructure provision. The ethos at the time favoured playing up the role of the private sector and downplaying that of governments. As the world's most powerful economic player, the US is able to influence global development philosophy and policy via the World Bank and other agencies. What this bias was to imply for infrastructure financing is dealt with elsewhere in this book, but one consequence was to hinder the mapping of global infrastructure needs. In more recent years, the advanced and emerging economies of the Group of 20 (G20) have made some progress in assessing global infrastructure needs and international consultants have added to the sum total of knowledge with private studies. Yet, the picture still lacks sharp focus and detail.

In the years and decades that followed the publication of the World Bank report, it became increasingly obvious that the task of providing the world with basic infrastructure was not going to be accomplished without substantial public sector inputs — financial and otherwise. A number of key events subsequent to the publication of the report underlined the fallacy of purely "market-driven" approaches to meeting the infrastructure deficit.

The emergence of China as a leading economic power and the success of the state-dominated economy in equipping itself with infrastructure needed to support dramatic growth (in the areas of transportation and energy especially) began to cast doubts on the so-called Washington Consensus ideas that encouraged the primacy of private enterprise over public enterprise. These deficiencies became increasingly obvious as infrastructure investment stagnated in leading Western economies, and more so in 2013 when China first announced its Belt and Road Initiative (BRI) to achieve infrastructural connectivity on a near-global scale.

The eruption of the Global Financial Crisis in 2008 had earlier exposed the weakness of financial systems that were focussed too much on short-term gains rather than long-term investments in areas such as infrastructure. After that, a series of disasters involving the collapse of major highway bridges in the US and Italy (and a tunnel collapse in Japan) highlighted the deteriorating state of the Western infrastructure.

As a result of all this, international awareness has grown of the need for a better understanding of infrastructure needs — a need reinforced by recognition of the impact that climate change will have on infrastructure and the necessity of adapting project designs accordingly. As noted, governments — those of the G20 advanced and emerging economies in particular — have finally begun to assume the task of preparing a world map of infrastructure needs, while the World Bank has retreated largely to the sidelines. The Washington Consensus is no longer all-pervasive, and a more realistic view is being taken of the role that governments will need to play in shaping infrastructure provision.

The nearest approach thus far to a world infrastructure atlas has come from the Global Infrastructure Hub (GIH), established in Sydney in 2014 under the auspices of the G20 advanced and emerging economies (see Fig. 2.1).The fact that the initiative was

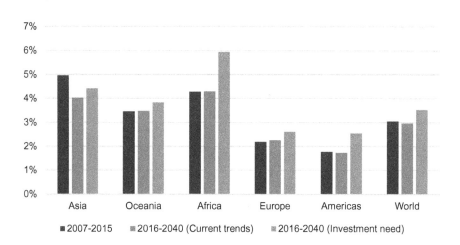

Figure 2.1.   Africa is Infrastructure-Hungry.

Source: Oxford Economics (2017). Global Infrastructure Outlook. Oxford. Licensed from the Global Infrastructure Hub Ltd under a Creative Commons Attribution 3.0 Australia License.

undertaken by the G20 rather than by the Group of Seven (G7) Western nations, which has been in existence for decades, is significant. While the advanced economies had been seemingly content to rely on orthodox approaches to infrastructure, emerging economies (China especially) brought new thinking to the need for a more systematic and comprehensive approach.

The Global Infrastructure Hub (GIH) is (in its own words) "the only organisation dedicated solely to infrastructure in developed and emerging markets." It works in collaboration with governments, the private sector, multilateral development banks, and other international institutions to "promote an enabling environment that will allow the identification and development of infrastructure projects that are high-quality, resilient, sustainable, and needed in a rapidly-evolving world" (Global Infrastructure Hub, n.d.).

The GIH has produced (in cooperation with Oxford Economics, an organisation specialising in global forecasting and quantitative analysis) a Global Infrastructure Outlook report. This document, published in 2017, followed the appearance of somewhat more limited studies published by international consultancies, such as McKinsey and PWC. But even the GIH study, which covers 50 of the 185 countries in the world, still falls rather short of being a global infrastructure atlas.

Prior to the publication of these studies, information had been scanty (rather like the efforts of early cartographers at mapping the world) on global infrastructure needs. The so-called league tables of countries with the best infrastructure (published by the World Economic Forum (WEF)) had placed Hong Kong and Singapore as co-equal near the top in terms of current infrastructure endowments. Switzerland topped some tables in terms of infrastructure quality while Japan also ranked high, along with European nations, such as the Netherlands, Finland, France, and Austria. By contrast, the United States was placed only 15th for railroad infrastructure and 14th for quality of roads in a WEF study. The UK also ranked low while Asian countries such as South Korea, Taiwan, and Malaysia were placed well ahead.

These reports made no attempt to assess future needs. The GIH report went considerably further, however, in quantifying the amounts and types of infrastructure spending that the world needs in the coming years and decades. It indicated an awareness of the fact that there is a problem, whereas the assumption in the past had been that the problem could be "left to the market," an attitude which had long hindered attempts to assess the true size and nature of the problem. How much the public and private sectors can be expected to contribute respectively to the financing of infrastructure remains unanswered, however, and this book suggests that a rebalancing of effort in favour of the public sector will be required.

The GIH study covered 50 countries of the world (in Asia, the Americas, Europe, and Oceania as well as Africa) which together account for some 85 per cent of the global gross domestic product (GDP). They consist of 15 low- and lower middle-income, 18 middle-income, and 17 high-income economies. The study looked at seven infrastructure sectors — roads, railways, airports, seaports, electric power generation and transmission, water supply, and telecommunications. Among these, electricity supply and roads will together account for more than two-thirds of the global needs in the coming decades, followed at some distance by telecommunications, rail, water, and, after that (again at some distance), by port and airport development.

The report estimated global infrastructure investment needs at US\$94 trillion between 2016 and 2040, although this sum will increase by US\$3.5 trillion if the world is to meet the United Nations Sustainable Development Goals in areas such as electricity and water supply. This means that by 2040, global spending on infrastructure will need to reach US$3.8 trillion annually. This figure is 67 per cent more (in real or inflation-adjusted terms) than what was spent in the year 2015. The report also suggested that if lower-spending countries wish to "raise their game to match their best-performing peers," overall infrastructure investment will need to reach US$4.6 trillion by 2040. This is US$880 billion more annually by 2040 than what is being spent at present.

Assessing infrastructure needs is not an easy task. It is a qualitative as well as a quantitative exercise because what some people define as "needs," others prefer to call "wishes." As the GIH said in its report, "even in countries with similar levels of economic development, policymakers may have very different objectives in providing infrastructure based on demand from citizens, economic expediency and political outlook."

This might affect how much a government prioritises rail over road connectivity or transport investment as a whole over other needs, such as providing access to clean water. The study made comparisons across countries to determine the investment that each country is likely to make in line with the current trends under a basic scenario and under a "needs" scenario if they increase spending to match that of their best-performing peers. Even if mapping infrastructure stocks and forecasting future investment needs can never be an exact science, the GIH report at least provided an order of magnitude.

Asian nations are currently big spenders on infrastructure and are expected to remain that way in the foreseeable future (see Table 2.1). They account for nearly 60 per cent of global spending on infrastructure and they will continue to account for 55 per cent between now and 2040. This might appear to suggest that Asia is lagging in infrastructure investment and that it needs to catch up. But Asia's ongoing needs for big spending is in fact linked to the region's dramatic economic growth in recent decades and the need

Table 2.1.   The Asian Equation.

Region/ Subregion	Projected Annual GDP Growth	2030 UN Population Projection (billion)	2030 Projected GDP per Capita (2015 US$)	Baseline Estimates			Climate-adjusted Estimates**		
				Investment Needs	Annual Average	Investment Needs as % of GDP	Investment Needs	Annual Average	Investment Needs as % of GDP
Central Asia	3.1	0.096	6,202	492	33	6.8	565	38	7.8
East Asia	5.1	1.503	18,602	13,781	919	4.5	16,062	1,071	5.2
South Asia*	6.5	2.059	3,446	5,477	365	7.6	6,347	423	8.8
Southeast Asia	5.1	0.723	7,040	2,759	184	5.0	3,147	210	5.7
The Pacific	3.1	0.014	2,2889	42	28	8.2	46	3.1	9.1
Asia and the Pacific	**5.3**	**4.396**	**9,277**	**22,551**	**1,503**	**5.1**	**26,166**	**1,744**	**5.9**

Note: *Pakistan and Afghanistan are included in South Asia. **Climate charge adjusted figures include climate mitigation and climate proofing costs, but do not include other adaptation costs, especially those associated with sea level rise.

Source: Asian Development Bank (2017). Meeting Asia's Infrastructure Needs. Manila. © ADB. DOI: 10.22617/FLS168388-2. Licensed under a Creative Commons Attribution 3.0 IGO License.

to underpin a continuation of this dynamic trend by continuing to invest heavily in infrastructure. There is also the fact that Asia is the world's most populous region and still needs to raise the living standards of many millions of its people.

In a report published in the same year (2017) as the GIH study, the Asian Development Bank (ADB) said that developing Asia (excluding more advanced economies, such as Japan and South Korea as well as Hong Kong, Taiwan, and Singapore) would need to invest US$26 trillion in the period from 2016 to 2030 or US$1.7 trillion per year if the region is to maintain its growth momentum, eradicate poverty, and respond to climate change.

Of the total, US$14.7 trillion would be for power and US$8.4 trillion for transport while investments in telecommunications would reach US$2.3 trillion and water and sanitation investment would need US$800 billion (see Table 2.2). These estimates were more than double the US$750 billion which the ADB published in 2009 (Asian Development Bank, 2017). A major factor behind the increase in spending needs was "the continued rapid growth forecast for the region, which generates new infrastructure demand," the ADB said, along with the inclusion of climate-related investments and the fact that the number of countries covered in the report rose from 32 to 45.

Designing infrastructure that is capable of withstanding the effects of climate change, for example, highways and railways, bridges, and port facilities that can weather the impact of more frequent wind damage and inundation, is clearly going to face much of the world with a major challenge in the coming years. The ADB built this into its calculations and raised its spending assessments accordingly.

Without climate change mitigation and adaptation costs, the estimate of total Asian spending needs in the period from 2016 to 2030 is US$22.6 trillion in total or US$1.5 trillion per year. If the wider impacts of climate change (for example, a switch from fossil

Table 2.2.   Asia's Needs by Sector.

Sector	Baseline Estimates			Climate-adjusted Estimates			Climate-related Investments (Annual)	
	Investment Needs	Annual Average	Share of Total	Investment Needs	Annual Average	Share of Total	Adaptation	Mitigation
Power	11,689	779	51.8	14,731	982	56.3	3	200
Transport	7,796	520	34.6	8,353	557	31.9	37	—
Telecommunications	2,279	152	10.1	2,279	152	8.7	—	—
Water and Sanitation	787	52	3.5	802	53	3.1	1	—
Total	**22,551**	**1,503**	**100.0**	**26,166**	**1,744**	**100.0**	**41**	**200**

Note: — denotes not applicable.
Source: Asian Development Bank (2017). Meeting Asia's Infrastructure Needs. Manila. ©ADB. DOI: 10.22617/FLS168388-2. Licensed under a Creative Commons Attribution 3.0 IGO License.

fuels to alternative forms of energy, with consequent redundancy of existing facilities) are factored in, spending estimates for infrastructure in Asia could be inflated even above the ADB's upper calculation. The same applies, obviously, to other areas of the world.

What stands out about Asia compared to other regions of the world — developed and developing countries alike — is that while its collective infrastructure spending needs are the highest, Asia is forecast to have a relatively small "investment gap" of just 10 per cent — meaning the gap between forecast needs for infrastructure spending and amounts that are already being spent at present. What is also significant is that in Asia governments are the biggest providers of infrastructure and this is one reason why infrastructure spending is at such levels in the region.

As the Global Infrastructure Hub has noted, "(the) picture is very different in other regions of the world." In the 11 countries of the Americas covered by the GIH study (Chile, Canada, the United states, Uruguay, Peru, Brazil, Ecuador, Argentina, Paraguay, Mexico, and Colombia) which rely considerably more on private sector investment in infrastructure, the gap between what is being spent now on infrastructure and what will be needed in the period to 2040 is forecast to be nearly five times as great as that in Asia at 47 per cent. In Africa, the gap is estimated at 39 per cent, while in Europe it is expected to be 16 per cent and in Oceania 10 per cent.

China is a polar opposite; rapid economic development in China over the past decade, as the GIH has noted, has been accompanied by a huge programme of infrastructure investment, such that between 2007 and 2015 China accounted for almost 30 per cent of all global infrastructure investment. The rate of investment is expected to be moderate in the coming decades, in line with the pattern for overall investment within the Chinese economy. China is expected to maintain a similar share of global infrastructure investment relative to

GDP well into the future. Under the current trends, China's infrastructure is forecast by the GIH to be slightly over US$26 trillion, or US$1.1 trillion per year in the period up to 2040. Given China's strong recent infrastructure investment performance, relatively little uplift in investment is required for China to match the performance of its top-performing peers.

Outside of China, "Asia" (defined by the GIH to include Japan, South Korea, Singapore, Thailand, Malaysia, Kazakhstan, Azerbaijan, India, Indonesia, Bangladesh, Vietnam, the Philippines, Pakistan, Myanmar, and Cambodia as well as Turkey, Jordan, and Saudi Arabia) is forecast to invest just under US$20 trillion in infrastructure between 2016 and 2040, although this increases to US$22.4 trillion under the "needs" scenario of performance. India will require the next largest infrastructure spending in the Asian region after China at nearly US$4.5 trillion, followed by Japan at US$3.8 trillion, Indonesia at US$1.7 trillion, and South Korea at US$1.4 trillion.

Behind Asia, the Americas (defined to include the US, Canada, Uruguay, Chile, Paraguay, Peru, Brazil, Colombia, Ecuador, Argentina, and Mexico) are forecast to be the next biggest spenders on infrastructure between now and 2040. The United States of course dominates the Americas overwhelmingly in terms of the size of its economy, which accounts for 95 per cent of regional GDP. The GIH report estimated infrastructure spending in the US between the years 2016 and 2040 at US$12.4 trillion in order to accommodate the expected economic and demographic growth during this period.

Based on the current spending trends, however, the US will likely invest only US$8.5 trillion, according to the GIH study. This again underlines the difficulty that the world's leading market economies have in directing funds into infrastructure, as shown also by the problems that President Donald Trump has had in trying to promote a US$1 trillion infrastructure renewal programme for the US.

The US is expected to continue emphasising highway infrastructure over railways, with road and electricity infrastructure accounting for three-quarters of the total while ports are being relatively neglected. In other countries of the Americas, beyond the US, combined investment is expected to amount to some US$5 trillion between now and 2040, although the real needs may be US$7.8 trillion if "needs" to match peers are factored in. As in the US, investment in roads is expected to take priority in the Americas.

In Europe, the GIH estimated that investment spending on infrastructure will total US$12.8 trillion in the period up to 2040, measured across nine countries (France, the UK, Italy, Germany, Spain, Poland, Croatia, Russia, and Romania) that together account for 70 per cent of regional GDP. But under the "investment needs" scenario, total spending would rise to US$14.8 trillion. Unlike the US, Europe tends to dedicate more investment to railways than to roads and the proportion going to telecommunications is also relatively high.

As a relatively mature infrastructure market, Europe tends to invest less in infrastructure as a proportion of GDP than regions which include more low- and middle-income countries, the GIH report noted. Europe invested just 2.2 per cent of GDP in infrastructure between 2007 and 2015, which is the second lowest proportion among all regions covered in the study. Overall, meeting Europe's infrastructure needs appears to be affordable, though increased spending will be required in certain sectors such as road and rail, the GIH concluded. France and Germany, in particular, have "very high-quality infrastructure in place across most sectors," the report found.

Africa's infrastructure spending (measured across nine countries — Angola, South Africa, Ethiopia, Tanzania, Senegal, Kenya, Morocco,

Egypt, and Nigeria represent 60 per cent of the continent's GDP) is projected to be US$4.3 trillion between now and 2040. This would rise to a total of US$6 trillion if African countries were able to raise their performance on infrastructure investment to that of their best-performing peers. In view of Africa's high poverty levels, most infrastructure investment tends to go to utilities like electricity, water, and sewage while road and rail infrastructure receive lower allocations.

As the scale and scope of the global infrastructure challenge comes (slowly) into closer focus, the greater the needs are seen to be in everything from highways, bridges, and railways to energy and water systems. Meanwhile, cost estimates go ever higher as infrastructure needs are better measured and as the necessity of adapting systems to cope with climate change are better appreciated. The necessity for better coordination of national programmes is also increasing as cross-border initiatives such as China's Belt and Road scheme and alternative regional undertakings emerge.

CHAPTER 3

INFRASTRUCTURE AND HOW THE WEST WAS LOST

The failure, so far, of Western nations to launch bold new infrastructure ventures on the scale of China's Belt and Road Initiative, or even to renew and maintain the existing infrastructure, is not only due to a lack of imagination but also due to the fact that those nations are unable to appreciate the importance of infrastructure. It is worth noting that the economic priorities and financial systems in Western societies have evolved in such a way so as to limit the ability to finance long-term capital investment of both public and private sectors of the economy. The roots of this problem go deep, but they are traceable to the recent evolution of capitalism in Western societies from a system where finance was formerly viewed as a "means to an end" to one where it has become more of an end in itself. Infrastructure has become a casualty of market economies that often appear to reward "financial engineering" more than they do physical engineering and construction.

When finance becomes an industry in itself, individuals and companies can become more concerned with making money than with making things, whether these "things" are manufactured goods or public goods like infrastructure. The consumer becomes king, and policy tends to stress consumption above other goals. In such situations, long-term investment tends to be sacrificed to short-term profit while resources are disproportionally directed toward financial services. State-run systems or "command economies" such as those of China's have different priorities that generally favour long-term capital investment projects. This is not to suggest that a Socialist reorientation is necessary in Western economies in order to support infrastructure. Rather, it is a wake-up call to policymakers in market economies on the need to re-order financial priorities and systems so that savings can be channelled into strengthening the physical foundations and growth potential of the economy.

There are other reasons why Western nations do not invest more in infrastructure. One has to do with the fact that Western economies are usually democracies where political leaders are sensitive to the need to deliver results within a framework of short-term electoral cycles. Infrastructure investment requires a long-term vision that can take many years to show results and for projects to pay for themselves. Western politicians cannot afford to be visionaries, and the grand gestures that characterized infrastructure building in past centuries have gone out of fashion.

Japan was one among the post-war leaders in building the basic infrastructure that underpinned the nation's manufacturing and export success. At present, Japan is influenced more by market economy principles and is wary of being seen to emphasise public investment. Some argue that Japan has over-invested in infrastructure such as the nation's Shinkansen high-speed rail networks, but such systems have strong potential for export to countries that are becoming aware of the need for modern and sophisticated transportation systems. China's approach to infrastructure stands in stark contrast to that of market economies. Its socialist system works well to support infrastructure investment. The government controls a major part of financial resources, via state-owned business enterprises and banks. Foreign exchange earnings from a myriad Chinese export enterprises serve as a huge pool of reserves from which the central government can draw.

However, outside of 'command' economies (China's for example) governments struggle, owing to a lack of control over funds that might be used to improve infrastructure. This is a critical factor and is likely to be overlooked when it comes to understanding why market economies apparently lack the will or ability to invest sufficiently in infrastructure. There is no shortage of money in the international financial system, and yet, from the point of view of infrastructure financing, the money is "in the wrong place." An estimated US$120 trillion is held by institutional investors such as pension fund providers, insurance companies, and the like. This is equal to more than 40 times the current global annual spending on infrastructure and is roughly equal to the global annual GDP. But the private sector is too fragmented in its composition and aims to forge a consensus on infrastructure investment.

Financial systems in market economies are not geared to channel private savings into infrastructure. Governments are still the principal source of finance for infrastructure and make use of taxes and other official revenues to serve the needs of the people. Yet, public investment in infrastructure is at a historic low in advanced economies (see Figure 3.1) and, while the private sector does finance roughly one half of all infrastructure investments in advanced nations, the deficit or "gap" between supply and demand continues to widen. For all the discussions that have taken place over many years about the need for the private sector to step up and do more by way of infrastructure financing, capital markets have proved to be unwilling or are unable to supply funds on anything like the scale needed — as discussed elsewhere in this book. Institutional investors, such as pension funds, life insurance companies, sovereign wealth funds, and private equity groups that

Figure 3.1.   It's a Jungle.
Source: neasecartoons.com. Cartoon by Steven Nease. Used with permission.

collect the bulk of private savings, are often unwilling to take the perceived risk of investing these funds in infrastructure projects.

The argument here is that governments in market economies should play a much bigger role in infrastructure financing, not by directing more tax revenues into this critical sector but for example by guaranteeing infrastructure project bonds so that institutional investors are willing to buy them on a much larger scale than that available at present. This could involve a significant increase in contingent liabilities on the public sector, but because of the taxes that they levy and revenue they generate from the other streams, governments are equipped to take a longer term view of risk than private sector institutions. The returns that infrastructure projects yield over time would justify the role played by the government as a guarantor. This could supply the "missing link" or missing channel for directing the private savings of market economies into infrastructure.

At what point in time did advanced economies go wrong in their approach to infrastructure? They were acutely mindful of the need for infrastructure renewal in the immediate post-World War II decades, both in war-ravaged Europe, where every form of transport and communications network along with energy grids had been destroyed, and also in America, which had escaped the direct ravages of war. The post-war period saw high and sustained levels of economic growth, full employment, and rising living standards in the West. It was a time of very strong public investment in infrastructure, education, and welfare, paid for or subsidised by relatively high and progressive taxation. Western European countries received resources worth US$130 billions (equivalent to 1 per cent of the GDP of the United States at the time) in the period from 1948 to 1952 under the US Marshall Plan. Much of this was devoted to infrastructure renewal while in the US itself the Highway Act of 1956 provided US$26 billion — the largest public works expenditure in the history of the US — to build more than 64,000 kilometres of federal roads to link together all parts of the country.

The two decades following World War II have been called the Golden Age of Capitalism, "a period of economic prosperity" extending from 1945 to the early 1970s. By the end of the 1970s, however, the post-war "Keynesian Consensus", which had encouraged distributive policies via fiscal stimulus and other means, paved the way for economic "neo-liberalism" under which 19th-century ideas associated with *laissez-faire* economic liberalism bounced back into fashion. This was manifested in privatisation, deregulation, and free-trade policies along with reductions in government spending aimed at increasing the role of the private sector in the economy. Market-based philosophies brought with them a paradigm shift away from the post-war Keynesian Consensus and came to be associated with an alternative "Washington Consensus."

This term was used originally to define a set of economic policies for developing countries, but it later came to embrace broader neo-liberal economic thinking. Aside from dictating a consensus approach by multilateral institutions toward development in emerging nations, Washington Consensus ideas became associated with market principles and in particular with the private enterprise-favouring policies of US President Ronald Reagan and British Prime Minister Margaret Thatcher. The anti-government mantra of that era also became orthodoxy under the former US president Bill Clinton and the then UK Prime Minister Tony Blair.

All this had a strong impact upon infrastructure. An ideological prejudice in favour of private sector initiatives and against the public sector came to dominate Western official thinking, and governments felt justified in reducing their focus on critical national investments. This proved to be a false step. As the Asian Development Bank Institute has noted, "governments were irrationally exuberant in their expectations of the private sector's ability to create infrastructure out of thin air" (Yoshino, Helble, & Abidhadjaev, 2018). Private investment in infrastructure did appear to take off for a while in the run up to the new millennium in both advanced and emerging economies. But this momentum was created by privatisation of the existing infrastructure assets — a process launched in Britain by Prime Minister Margaret Thatcher in the 1990s, supported by President Ronald Reagan, and copied in some parts of the developing world such as Latin America.

This momentum quickly faded, however, once the higher revenue-generating and more profitable public assets had been divested (or the "family silver sold off" as some charged). These assets were sold precisely because their strong revenues made them marketable. Had they been retained under government control, their revenues might have helped to subsidize other public utilities. Privatisation has largely not worked. It has often resulted in sub-standard services being offered to the public at higher prices than under state ownership.

Then came the Global Financial Crisis in 2008–2009, and private investment in infrastructure slumped once again. An unremarked irony at the time was that the lack of infrastructure bonds and the other long-term financial instruments in many advanced economies helped fuel the global crisis by diverting investment into securitised assets and other financial derivatives. Had infrastructure bonds been available widely at that time, there would have been an ample supply of long-term financial instruments to absorb savings. Instead, a short-term investment ethic was allowed to triumph over longer-term vision, and it helped to create a spiral of financial destruction.

Authorities were effectively panicked into launching monetary and (some) fiscal stimuli during the Global Financial Crisis in order to avert systemic financial failure and to prevent the 1930s Great Depression from being repeated. Central banks created trillions of dollars of new liquidity in the banking system in order to prevent further failures after the Lehman Brothers collapse and to avert a freeze-up in global trade and investment. Even so, the creation of this new financial liquidity and the consequent plunge in interest rates (to zero or even negative levels in some cases) failed to stimulate new long-term investment, with business confidence remaining at a very low level for a very long time.

And with the emphasis being more on monetary easing than on fiscal stimulus, Keynesian spending on the scale of early post-war initiatives failed to reappear.

The global economy slowed dramatically along with a slowdown in world trade. Capital investment flagged and growth stayed on the floor for nearly a decade. China, however, emerged as a beacon of hope in the encircling gloom. The Chinese government applied massive infrastructural and other fiscal stimulus to the nation's economy, helping fuel growth in other emerging economies and acted as a dynamo to offset the slump in advanced economies.

There was talk in mature economies of the need for new Keynesian stimulus, and some governments did enact measures to stabilise aggregate demand. But with a decrease in the tax revenues and an increase in the demand for social spending, government deficits and debt levels rose to new peacetime highs, requiring significant and sustained fiscal consolidation. As the European Investment Bank (EIB) commented at the time, "the need for fiscal consolidation is here to stay [and] this will affect government investment significantly, including in infrastructure"(Strauss, 2010).

To date, public investment in infrastructure is at a historic low in advanced economies and, while the private sector does nowadays finance roughly one half of all infrastructure investment in advanced nations, the deficit or "gap" between supply and demand continues to widen. In developing and emerging economies as a whole, the public sector finances 70 per cent of all projects while only 20 per cent are financed by the private sector, and the remaining 10 per cent are financed by multilateral development banks (McKinsey Global Institute, 2016).

Infrastructure investment has actually declined as a share of gross domestic product in 11 of the G20 group of advanced and emerging economies since the global financial crisis a decade ago, despite glaring gaps in infrastructure provision and years of debate about the importance of shoring up foundational systems. Cutbacks have occurred in the European Union, the United States, Russia, and Mexico while investment increased in Canada, Turkey, and South Africa only. According to the consultants McKinsey, the world currently invests US$2.5 trillion a year in transport, energy, and communications infrastructure but needs to increase this amount to at least US$3.3 trillion a year between now and 2030 in order to support the estimated economic growth between now and then.

The problems with infrastructure financing are by no means confined to advanced economies alone. In developing and emerging economies as a whole, the public sector finances 70 per cent of all projects while only 20 per cent are financed by the private sector, and the remaining 10 per cent are financed by multilateral development banks. These are impressive contributions by the governments of the developing countries in relation to the overall infrastructure spending but (with the notable exception of China) the infrastructure "gap" — financial and physical — in the developing world yawns wide. If the developing economies have anything to learn from their "advanced" counterparts, it is to not do things the Western way when it comes to infrastructure financing. They should not necessarily copy the Chinese model as well. There are "middle" ways.

CHAPTER 4

CHINA'S "BELT AND ROAD" — AN IMPERIAL HIGHWAY TO THE FUTURE?

China has been the first mover in an unfolding infrastructure revolution that has the potential to transform much of the face of the earth. New highway and rail networks are beginning to march across the Eurasian continent and beyond while parallel maritime "roads" link continents together in a global nexus of land and sea communications. These developments open up prospects for expanded commerce and industrial production, boosting economic growth and prosperity in the process. But like all innovations, the infrastructure revolution has the potential for both good and bad outcomes.

Just as German Autobahns opened the way for massive military movements in pre-World War II Europe, the "multi-modal" transport networks under construction now by China and others have the potential to spark conflicts. China's infrastructure revolution began at home. Once it began to modernise and open up its economy 40 years or so ago, China channelled huge amounts of state funds into infrastructure and now has what is described by experts as being among the best transportation infrastructure in the world. It has, for example, built vast networks of toll highways plus a high-speed rail network that is scheduled to stretch to 120,000 kilometres in length by 2020. There has also been huge investment in power generation and transmission. The pace of investment is forecast to remain high in the future, with a particular emphasis on urban renewal.

The Chinese economy has been the fastest growing in the world in recent decades and one of the defining features of that growth has been "massive development of physical infrastructure" (Chen, Matzinger, & Woetzel, 2013). There is, McKinsey suggested, "unidirectional causality from infrastructure development to output growth, justifying China's high spending on infrastructure development since the early nineties." Experience from China, the consultants added, "suggests that it is necessary to design an economic policy that improves physical infrastructure as well as human capital formation for sustainable economic growth in developing countries."

The Chinese government has also used substantial infrastructure spending to hedge against flagging economic growth. And it has charted equally ambitious plans for the future. The goal is to bring the entire nation's urban infrastructure up to the level of infrastructure in a middle-income country, while using increasingly efficient transport logistics to bind the nation together. As a result of its huge capital investment programme, McKinsey added, China now has a relatively modest infrastructure "investment gap" (the difference between investment needs and actual investment) of only 1.2 per cent of GDP — half the gap that exists in Asia overall and well below the level in many developed nations.

Reform has not stopped at China's borders. Now China is in the process of "exporting" its infrastructure revolution via the so-called "Belt and Road Initiative" (BRI), which aims at linking China directly with much of the rest of the world through an extensive network of land and sea routes (see Fig. 4.1). The first time the outside world

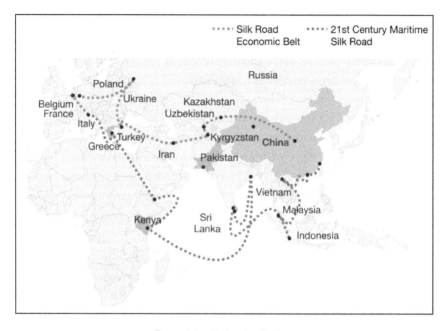

Figure 4.1.   By Land or By Sea.
Source: McKinsey Company. https://www.mckinsey.com/industries/capital-projects-and-infrastructure/our-insights/one-belt-and-one-road-connecting-china-and-the-world.

heard of this remarkable plan, which recalled the vision and "romance" of the historical "Silk Road" and the infrastructure feats of the ancient Roman Empire, was in 2013 when President Xi Jinping announced the creation of a semi-global network of road, rail, air, and sea linkages plus energy and communication networks. Xi's plan envisaged land and sea links stretching right across Asia and into Africa via the Middle East. This was later expanded to embrace Latin America and more far-flung regions of the world.

The grand design emerged during a visit by Xi to Central and Southeast Asia when he floated the idea of developing a "Silk Road Economic Belt and the 21st-Century Maritime Silk Road." Three routes were proposed — North, Central, and South. The northernmost would pass through Central Asia and Russia and into Europe; the Central route was proposed through Central and West

Asia to the Persian Gulf and the Mediterranean; and the southern route was intended to be built from China to Southeast Asia, South Asia, and the Indian Ocean. All this involved linkage stretching across no fewer than 70 countries. The plan envisaged the development of six major economic corridors, including the New Eurasian Land Bridge, the China–Mongolia–Russia corridor, the China–Central Asia–Western Asia corridor, the Indo-China Peninsula corridor, the China–Pakistan and Bangladesh corridor, and the China–India–Myanmar corridor. These are intended to involve construction of land, sea, and air linkages that would in turn attract "clusters" of industrial and business activities that would be served by new energy systems and information "highways".

Xi declared that China wished to "build bridges" between China and Europe — not simply metaphorical bridges but physical ones. Several years later in 2017 when the Belt and Road project was formally launched during a gathering of global leaders in Beijing, Xi waxed lyrical about what he had in mind. "Two thousand years ago," he said, "our ancestors trekking across vast steppes and deserts opened the transcontinental passage connecting Asia, Europe and Africa, known as the Silk Road. Navigating rough seas [they] created routes linking the East with the West — the maritime Silk Road." Great adventurers, Xi recalled, "including Du Huan of China, Marco Polo of Italy and Ibn Battuta of Morocco, left their footprints along these ancient routes. All this "enabled people of different civilisations, religions and races to interact and embrace each other with an open mind." The time had come, to re-create the Silk Road vision, he suggested.

Not everyone perceived Xi's vision in a favourable light. A more sceptical view saw the BRI as being not so much about promoting logistical and economic connectivity as part of a wider strategy, whereby China could become a regional hegemon capable of countering the United States–Japan alliance in this role. It was also viewed by some as a means to secure raw material and other inputs needed to feed China's massive industrial appetite and to secure global markets for its products. Whatever its true nature, the ambition of China's earth-girdling venture was masked from the outset by its rather dull title. Initially called "One Belt-One Road" or OBOR, the project was later renamed as an (equally uninspiring) Belt and Road Initiative. This was seen widely as being a disguised declaration of "infrastructure war" by China.

The romance of new highways and railroads cutting a path across vast plains, mountain ranges and borders — opening up new territory and opportunities in the process — is lost on many people. Yet, the BRI has since begun to turn some dreams into reality. It is creating new economic hinterlands and markets for China and its neighbours in the East, and for the whole of Europe in the West. Rail freight times are being cut dramatically as trains roll thousands of miles across Central Asia directly from China to Europe and back. Revival of the Silk Road concept is also providing a major boost for tourism in Central Asia and Western parts of China.

Even so, these positive aspects have been overshadowed to some extent by suspicion and doubt. Following its launch, some external critics began describing the BRI as an instrument of Chinese economic imperialism. They attacked the plan for the alleged lack of transparency and for the absence of representation by participating countries in decision making. In places as far apart as Sri Lanka and the Maldives to Pakistan, Greece and Italy, China has been accused of luring host nations along the Belt and Road routes to borrow heavily for infrastructure projects, making those countries incur huge debt in the process. They are then, according to this argument, forced to handover ownership of strategic assets such as seaports to China in return for debt relief or debt forgiveness.

Some of these criticisms are understandable. The BRI is not an "institution" as such, and countries that participate in its projects cannot become members of it in a legal sense. Nor can they participate in governance of the BRI, which is administered by several different Chinese government ministries. The nearest they can get to "joining" or influencing the scheme is to become members of the China-led Asian Infrastructure Investment Bank (AIIB), which has 100 member governments as shareholders and which is viewed by many as being a "Siamese twin" of the BRI.

Even this indirect option for influencing the policies of the BRI has appeared, however, to be limited by the fact that the AIIB has insisted initially on remaining at arm's length from the BRI, so as not to jeopardise the international credit ratings of the AIIB by linking it too closely with (sometimes controversial) Belt and Road projects. In March 2019, however, Italy became the first among the Group of Seven (G7) advanced nations to endorse Belt and Road projects in which the AIIB will be closely involved.

These involve development of the Italian port of Trieste, which has been of commercial and strategic significance since the days of the Holy Roman Empire. Other infrastructure and technology projects are involved in the China–Italy deal. China already has stakes in the ports of Venice and Genoa but the move by the BRI into Trieste accompanied by the AIIB is likely to lend enhanced legitimacy to both institutions. (China also owns the Port of Piraeus in Greece and has stakes in a dozen other European ports in the Netherlands, Belgium, Germany, and beyond.)

The BRI is dependent upon various sources within China for funding. Apart from tapping (so far to a limited extent) the AIIB which has a capital base of US$100 billion, the BRI is able to obtain funds through China's Silk Road Fund, which is based (like the AIIB) in Beijing and which has a capital of US$40 billion (OECD, 2018a). The fund is designed to channel private sector funds into the BRI. Yet another "pillar" of the BRI is the New Development Bank (or the so-called "BRICS" Bank), which is based in Shanghai and has a capital of US$50 billion. A host of other Chinese lending institutions including, chiefly, the China Development Bank and the Export–Import Bank of China also support the BRI.

China began aggressively signing bilateral deals with some of the 60 or more countries along the Belt and Road route shortly after the initiative was launched — and that was when rivalry began to emerge towards the basic concept. In 2015, the Japanese government announced a programme of the so-called "Quality Infrastructure Investment for Asia's Future," for which US$110 billion of Japanese official funding was promised (Ministry of Foreign Afairs of Japan, 2015). This seemed to be aimed at outbidding the US$100 billion capital pledged to the AIIB by its leading shareholders including the top three — China itself, India, and Russia. At the same time, the "quality" infrastructure tag adopted by Japan and others appeared to be designed to contrast favourably with China's image as a provider of lower quality and cheaper infrastructure.

Further stepping up rivalry with the BRI, Japanese Prime Minister Shinzo Abe and Indian Prime Minister Narendra Modi announced in 2016 a joint plan for an "Asia–Africa Growth Corridor" which looked remarkably similar to the BRI. The administration of US President Donald Trump also responded with a composite scheme for an "Indo-Pacific Business Forum" or consortium to be created in collaboration with Japan, India, and others to make joint investments in infrastructure and other projects across a region broadly similar to that covered by China's Belt and Road. The combat was then broadened and intensified further in 2018 when the US, together with Japan and Australia, announced the launch of a "Trilateral Partnership" to pursue infrastructure and other public projects in Asia using financial resources contributed by all three countries. By labelling this as an "Indo-Pacific" (rather than "Asia-Pacific") venture, the US sought to shift the centre of geo-economic and strategic gravity in Asia from China to a more Westerly orientation based on India. At the same time, Washington intentionally underlined the fact that the new initiatives by the Trilateral Partnership would focus on "market-led" economic development rather than on the state enterprise-led model of China.

In November 2019, the trilateral partners refined the name of their infrastructure cooperation to the "Blue Dot Network" in an apparent attempt to make it more easily identifiable as an alternative to China's Belt and Road Initiative. But as The Economist newspaper commented subsequently, the "financial muscle behind the [Blue Dot Network] looks puny in comparison" to the BRI.

Some do not see competition between the major infrastructure mega schemes as being necessarily wasteful or harmful. Having some competition for the Belt and Road is "good for China and good for the world," suggests Amar Bhattacharya, senior fellow at the Global Economy and Development Program at Brookings Institution in Washington. Even so, Bhattacharya is concerned that the huge infrastructure projects underway by rival powers are not being as closely coordinated as they should be at the global level. "Because of the nature of these investments, we should not be looking at them one project or one corridor at a time, but really as a system to see they really make sense," he argues. "There no evaluation of this kind which has been done. I really think that the World Bank and the IMF and the OECD and other international institutions ought to be able to say, 'what is the [overall] vision of connectivity?'"

In the same way that China's motives in launching the BRI have been questioned, the likely final size of the massive project has been challenged. A joint study by Japan's Nikkei Asian Review and The Banker magazine carried out and published in both journals in 2018 by Japan's *Nikkei Asian Review* and *The Banker Magazine* of the UK in collaboration with the Centre for Strategic and International Studies (CSIS) in Washington suggested that BRI is longer in dreams than in reality. The number of projects planned, underway, or completed at that time, the study suggested, was relatively small and "big numbers being floated for President Xi Jinping's signature foreign policy effort, the BRI, do not add up."

The study mapped US$4.5 billion worth of transport and energy projects in Hungary, Iran, Kazakhstan, Pakistan, Sri Lanka, Cambodia, Indonesia, and North Korea as having been completed and US$37 billion worth of projects in Bangladesh, Laos, Israel, Mongolia, Turkey, and the Ukraine as being "under construction" or "announced." The value of projects included in the joint study amounted to US$42 billion overall. "Without a clearer sense of the BRI's scale, it is difficult to assess its economic and strategic implications," the study concluded while also suggesting that the highest estimated spending for the BRI might have been inflated with the aim of "scoring political points for Beijing."

In June 2020, The Economist reported that, as a result of the COVID-19 pandemic, work had come to a halt on some BRI projects, while "a few" had been scrapped. Many loans made in connection with BRI projects "are on the brink of technical default as debtor countries hammered by COVID-19 seek to defer payments that are coming due," the report said ("Pandemic", 2020). Most of the troubled projects are reportedly in the energy sector. Views have been expressed meanwhile to the effect that China should consider converting loans made to BRI projects into equity, which would both ease the financial burden on debtor countries and clarify China's ownership of assets (such as land) needed to implement projects.

As with the BRI, controversy also dogged the launch of the AIIB. In an unprecedented move shortly after the formal launch of the AIIB and of the New Development Bank or "BRICS" bank in 2016, the established family of multilateral development banks led by the World Bank and others such as the Asian Development Bank (ADB) issued a joint statement warning borrowers against "new entrants" and implying that their lending and project standards could be sub-standard.

The statement did not mention any names, but it was clear that the AIIB and the BRICS bank (in which Brazil, Russia, India, China, and South Africa are the chief shareholders) were the focus of the warning.

The development bank "establishment" — many of whose members operate under the aegis of the United Nations — had already suggested that some of China's bilateral infrastructure lending to countries in Africa and elsewhere did not match global standards in matters such as environmental protection and safeguards against "over lending" to poorer countries. And, they had raised as a red flag the allegation that governance standards at the AIIB did not match their own standards, in that the Chinese bank did not have a resident board of directors from shareholding countries at AIIB headquarters. Such criticisms may have some validity, but it was difficult to separate them from the fact that established development banks were smarting from criticisms that Chinese officials had in turn levelled against them suggesting that bureaucratic inertia on the part of established lending institutions often led to long delays (sometimes many years) in approving the loans needed to finance infrastructure. China launched the Beijing-based AIIB with the promise that it would be less bound by red tape than other development banks and swifter in approving loans. Chinese officials also claimed that institutions such as the World Bank (*de facto* head of the multilateral development bank family) had become captives of civil society groups.

The ADB for one, taking a leaf out of the book of the World Bank, had made poverty reduction the "overarching objective" of its lending — a goal that China saw as vague and which has led to waste of resources on social objectives at the expense of building physical infrastructure. The AIIB insisted that it would not become a tool of civil society groups and NGOs (non-governmental organisations) and that its lending would be based on the economic needs of borrowers rather than on what outsiders judge to be "good" for them. The choice of the title of the Asia Infrastructure "Investment" (rather than "Development") Bank was deliberate in order to emphasise its focussed role on infrastructure rather than more nebulous development objectives.

A former ADB Vice President and alternate governor for China at the World Bank and now Chairman and President of the AIIB, Jin Liqun has insisted that the bank will be a "lean" institution in terms of the size of its staffing compared to some other multilateral institutions. He has demonstrated this principle by dispensing with resident executive directors at the bank. Jin stresses, however, the importance of the oversight exercised by the AIIB Board, whose role he says is strong despite the bank's different approach. Use of modern technology can ensure that our non-resident board has no less ready access to information about what is going on in the Bank than if its members were here on the premises. "Physically, Board members are scattered over the world; functionally, they remain close to the management and staff on a daily basis. This also allows us to save on costs, which ultimately benefits our shareholders."

Being lean does not stop at the non-residency of the Board, Jin argued to the author. "It means that, at its core, the bank will prioritise efficiency in all aspects of its business and operations. We are already seeing this implemented in various ways. We have adopted a measured approach to staffing, ensuring there is no [functional] redundancy. The AIIB will strive to remain a small organisation, relative to the size of its operations. The lean structure will be institutionalised as part of the corporate culture." And it is not just in improved efficiency that the AIIB can make a difference, he argues. China's economy, he notes, "continues to get bigger and now it is China's turn to do a bit for the rest of Asia and the world." China can, for example, demonstrate to others the value of infrastructure investment. "China's fast growth in virtually all sectors of the economy over the last three decades was preceded by infrastructure investment."

Jin is at pains to clarify the relationship between the AIIB and China's BRI. The BRI, he says, "is certainly is related to the AIIB but they are not the same thing. The AIIB is not created exclusively to finance [BRI] projects. The AIIB covers more broadly countries across the world. Generally speaking, we highlight the importance of regional connectivity. Those projects which are good for the borrowing country with positive spillovers across borders will certainly receive high priority. The projects we can consider should be financially sustainable, environmentally friendly, and socially acceptable."

Jin challenges the poverty-reduction focus of multilateral development banks. Poverty reduction, he argued has become a "poster child for the virtue of development banks but it is little more than that." Jin added that he had a "deep conviction that any poverty reduction programme in itself [would] not go far in making a difference to the livelihood of the poor." Broad-based economic and social development "is the ultimate solution for poverty reduction. Making poverty reduction the overarching objective will do nothing but restrict [development banks'] effectiveness." Radical rethinking is needed on these issues, Jin says while citing China's own impressive record on infrastructure building and poverty reduction. There is, he said, "empirical evidence of a link between infrastructure investment and economic growth." Largely owing to improved infrastructure, China managed to uplift more than 500 million people out of poverty by World Bank standards, and 600 million by China's standards, in little over two decades. The percentage of the population living in poverty meanwhile fell from 65 per cent in 1981 to 4 per cent in 2007.

Not everyone accepts China's claims that more pragmatic considerations should guide development bank lending. Among critics of this view is Masuhiro Kawai, former head of the Office of Regional Economic Integration at the ADB. While the ADB has a "vision" of reducing poverty across Asia, China's schemes appear designed to "enrich Chinese companies seeking projects overseas," Kawai suggested to the author. "China," he charged, "is setting up a major regional and international organisation without a vision. Any organisation should have clear vision. Otherwise [it] is going to benefit only China and Chinese construction companies."

China's approach nevertheless has its defenders beyond the realm of AIIB officials. One such is Yuqing Xing, a former professor of economics at the Graduate Institute for Policy Studies in Tokyo, who argues that China's launch of the BRI and the AIIB has already begun to influence policy thinking in key nations of the world. "There has been a 'catfish effect,'" he suggested to the author, meaning that competition from China's initiatives has provoked a change in attitudes elsewhere. "The Japanese government, the ADB, and the World Bank have all pledged to increase investment in infrastructure. Regardless of China's political and diplomatic motivations in setting up AIIB, the investment boom triggered by this move will surely promote regional economic development."

China can achieve its wider policy objectives through the AIIB, Xing suggests. It will, he says, "challenge the dominance of the World Bank and of the ADB in financing regional infrastructure projects and in transforming global economic governance from a US-led unipolar model to a multi-polar model." According to Xing, China will utilise the AIIB to achieve diplomatic, economic, and political objectives, such as providing multilateral aid, nurturing new markets, developing Chinese "soft power," and steering Asian regional cooperation and integration in addition to supporting the BRI. Global economic governance under the Bretton Woods system, he argues, has failed to recognise the progress and status of the Chinese economy, and China's efforts to increase its influence within the system have been fruitless. "Establishing a China-led multinational development bank can ensure China's multilateral aid serve its national interest best and develop its regional leadership."

Despite the hostility which initially greeted the launch of the AIIB and other new entrants to the sphere of development financing, many countries were eager to see China contribute some of its wealth (huge foreign exchange reserves, for example) to financing infrastructure. Apart from India and Russia, countries in Asia, Latin America, Africa, and the Middle East quickly joined the shareholding family at the AIIB. More importantly (and over the objections of the United States), a clutch of key European nations led by Britain also signed up to membership, leaving the United States and Japan as the only "holdouts" of any financial consequence. One factor behind this was eagerness on the part of many countries to become eligible to bid on lucrative AIIB infrastructure projects. Britain was also eager to act as a financing centre for Belt and Road projects. Meanwhile, cooperation "on the ground" between the AIIB and other multilateral development institutions has been remarkably close. The World Bank in effect ran the AIIB Treasury department for a time after the Chinese-led bank opened its doors in 2015 and also helped set up its IT systems. The World Bank also seconded other staff to the AIIB and co-financed its first project while the ADB offered similar assistance.

The BRI itself faces challenges, as admitted even by enthusiasts such as Northeast Asia expert and prominent academic Kent Calder Director of the Edwin O. Reischauer Center for East Asian Studies at Johns Hopkins University in a personal interview with the author in Tokyo in 2017 who finds the Chinese vision "exciting" while adding that "how practical and affordable it is may be a different matter." Despite such doubts, however, the twin strategies that Beijing has adopted by launching the BRI and the AIIB more or less in parallel and as mutually supporting entities suggest that China has a far better chance of pulling off such ambitious ventures than do other powers such as the United States or European nations. One reason for this is the problems market economies face in marshalling the billions of dollars of investment they need to build new transport, energy, and communications infrastructure or even to maintain the current infrastructure services. These problems are dealt with elsewhere in this book, but China appears to have found a way of combining state capitalism with global financial market access in order to finance the huge investments required for infrastructure. It is directing state funds into the BRI while also using the AIIB and the Silk Road Fund to attract money from international capital markets.

The significance of this potent combination appears to have escaped general notice — not least with regard to the role which the AIIB will play in giving institutional substance to the BRI, allowing countries involved in BRI projects to have a say in their implementation. As Yuqing Xing notes, China "will be able to use the AIIB as an institutional platform for discussion and coordination among member countries for facilitating the BRI." Thus, the AIIB will enable China to implement its strategy "not only in terms of financial support but also from the point of view of cross-country coordination."

As noted, there are political reasons why China has not appeared eager to highlight the role that the AIIB will play within the BRI. AIIB president Jin makes the point that his bank "covers more broadly countries across the world." His reluctance to link the two entities closely reflects the fact that the AIIB has some 100 countries among its shareholders, among which China is the largest. China effectively controls the AIIB, but it cannot be seen to be treating the institution as a "captive" lender to BRI projects. Likewise, China needs to be careful about devoting too much of its own war chest of foreign exchange reserves to financing BRI projects. At their peak around 2015, these reserves (invested largely US Treasury bonds) reached nearly US$4 trillion, but this has since declined to below US$3 trillion as China suffered capital outflows. In order to prevent BRI projects from eating up too much of the remaining hoard (which is invested mainly in US Treasury securities), China has begun denominating its own loans to the BRI in renminbi rather than in dollars.

In the same way that the AIIB needs to avoid a perception of being "too close" to the BRI, China's government needs to avoid creating an overdependence on the state for infrastructure financing, McKinsey has suggested. It argues that government-led infrastructure development in China has resulted in "heavy dependence on a single source of financing [and this] has increased government debt significantly." The Chinese model "is not sustainable" in the long term, the consultancy argues.

A critical issue for both the BRI and the AIIB is whether the United States and Japan will continue to distance themselves from these key initiatives or choose to cooperate with them. The closest the US has come so far to open confrontation with the BRI (and by implication with the AIIB also) was in October 2018 when US Vice President Mike Pence launched a strong verbal attack on (unnamed) nations that, he said, seek to ensnare countries that host infrastructure projects in a "debt trap" which forces them into strategic subservience to the lender.

Both US President Donald Trump and Japanese Prime Minister Shinzo Abe have the reputation of being "nationalist" leaders who are not eager to cede credit to China for its economic and strategic emergence on the world stage and far less to assist that process by endorsing Chinese initiatives like the BRI and the AIIB. The fact that joint US–Japan initiatives have been proposed to create alternative models to the BRI — ones that promote private over state enterprise — are evidence of this.

The Trump administration has also been instrumental in installing a new president at the World Bank in the person of David Malpass who is expected to push the bank into a more proactive role as a global lender in the face of rising competition from the AIIB. All this appears to point to the emergence of two new major players on the global infrastructure stage — the AIIB-backed BRI on the one side and a World Bank-supported US–Japan–Australia Trilateral Partnership (with India also closely involved) on the other side. This appears to rule out the possibility of either the United States or Japan applying for membership of the AIIB in the foreseeable future, unless they feel they can straddle the growing geo-strategic divide on infrastructure by doing so. If that divide does continue to widen through stepped-up competition between the world's major economies, then at least the infrastructure "financing gap" may benefit from having more resources directed from both sides to help close it.

CHAPTER 5

BELT AND ROAD RIVALS EMERGE

Asia is becoming the main theatre of global "infrastructure wars" as leading Asia-Pacific powers — chiefly the United States, China, and Japan plus India and Australia — battle for economic and strategic supremacy in the world's most populous and potentially most prosperous region. One casualty of this combat (apart from the obvious danger of physical friction developing among regional powers) is that attempts are being made to divide the region into two centres of economic and strategic power — the Asia-Pacific and the Indo-Pacific, with an emerging and thrusting China dominating the first and an essentially defensive United States leading the second, together with Japan and others.

These major powers have become locked into competition on land and at sea to establish what are sometimes referred to rather blandly as economic "corridors," but which in reality are avenues for the projection of strategic as well as economic power through the control of key terrestrial highways and sea lanes. The full dimensions and significance of this competition and the conflicts that it could generate are potentially huge, and yet, so far, they appear to be less appreciated among many Western nations.

In essence, China is attempting via its Belt and Road Initiative (BRI) to link itself overland to Europe (via Central Asia) as well as to the Middle East and Africa and beyond, greatly extending its power projection in the process. The US, along with Japan and other strategic allies, is meanwhile intent upon turning the Indian Ocean and Arabian Sea, along with countries bordering these oceans and stretching (from South and Southeast Asia to East Africa) into a new "centre" of the Asian world. The US is working principally with Japan, Australia, and India in this regard, seeing a quadrilateral alliance as a means to fend off the Chinese challenge.

In another development of economic and strategic importance, Russia is meanwhile anxious to exploit the trade and other potential of the newly opened Arctic sea routes linking Japan (in summer) with Norway and Sweden. The logistical and commercial shifts implied by all this competition are enormous. For example, under the Belt and Road scheme, large volumes of freight that have traditionally travelled by sea from China, Japan, South Korea, and other parts of East Asia to Europe could be diverted across Central Asia and from there on across the Atlantic to the US. There are already two Eurasian rail routes in operation that make this possible, plus another one that links China with Siberia.

China's emergence as a major player on the economic (and increasingly military) scene has heightened the friction between Beijing and Tokyo and this in turn has prompted Japan to seek closer ties with India and Australia while at the same time strengthening its strategic and commercial links with the United States. This conflict is assuming new and wider dimensions as the players seek to construct competing "architectures" of infrastructure linking themselves more closely with one another and with the rest of the world.

After China made the initial announcement of its BRI in 2013, Japan responded by exploring the possibility of developing a similar transcontinental network with India and other partners, to be known as the Asia–Africa Growth Corridor or AAGC. The battle for economic and geo-strategic "spheres of influence" then became apparent with the launch in August 2018 of the US government-led Indo-Pacific Business Forum. This was quickly followed by the announcement of a "Trilateral Partnership" among US, Japan, and Australia aimed at marshalling public and private investment from the three countries into Asian infrastructure and other major projects. It also signalled an attempt to reassert the primacy of US-style private enterprise over Chinese state capitalism. Initially, the chief aim of the BRI appeared to be to link the Chinese mainland to the Continent of Europe by means of rail and road links running across Central Asia. This would bring together a European industrial heartland that is shifting closer to the east of the continent with a Chinese industrial complex that is moving to the west of the country. At that point, plans to extend the BRI to the Middle East and North Africa appeared to be little more than a "sideshow."

For Japan, however, whose economy is highly dependent upon trans-Pacific trade with the US and which has long used Southeast Asia as its economic hinterland, the proposed geographical reach of China's grand plan was more alarming. As Tokyo saw it, China was not only proposing the creation of new Eurasian transport links that would challenge the dominance of Pacific and other maritime trade routes but also planning to acquire a network of ports and harbours stretching to the Indian Ocean and into the Middle East and Africa and beyond. From the Japanese perspective, this suggested that China could come to control not only a giant slice of global commerce and trade but also access to militarily strategic ports and harbours.

This threat appeared to become greater with the Trump administration's apparent preference for neo-isolationist and mercantilist policies. In order to counter this perceived threat, Japanese Prime Minister Shinzo Abe stepped up diplomacy with the Indian Prime Minister Narendra Modi so as to get Delhi more closely involved in a plan aimed at thwarting what Japan saw as a power grab by Beijing.

The Indo-Japanese response initially took the form of stepped-up security cooperation but soon a joint proposal emerged for creating the so-called Asia–Africa Growth Corridor. This plan envisaged creating a network of infrastructure links extending from East Asia to Africa via the Middle East and in which the two countries would be the principal partners (see Fig. 5.1).

This plan envisaged creating a network of infrastructure links extending from East Asia to Africa via the Middle East and in which the two countries would be the principal partners.

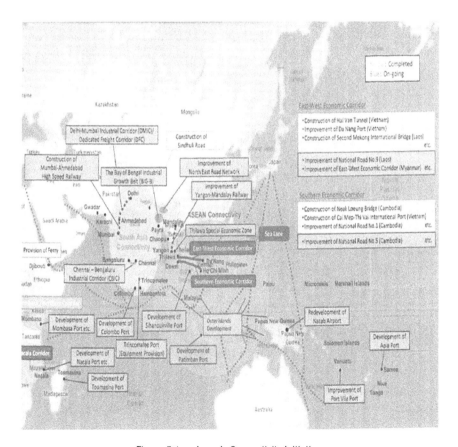

Figure 5.1.   Japan's Connectivity Initiative.
Source: Japanese Ministry of Foreign Affairs.

As with China's BRI, the AAGC envisaged not just a transcontinental network of highways but also maritime facilities stretching from East Asia to the Middle East and Africa. The AAGC plan appeared to be driven as much by strategic and security aims (through control over access to key ports in the Indian Ocean and elsewhere) as by a vision of global connectivity. The basic outline of a "growth corridor" emerged in November 2016 when Modi and his Japanese counterpart met in Delhi. This meeting was followed in May 2017 by a joint vision document published by India's Research and Information System for Developing Countries together with the Jakarta-based Economic Research Institute for ASEAN and East Asia (ERIA) and the Institute of Developing Economies at the Japan External Trade Organization (JETRO). Tokyo and Delhi appeared to regard the scheme as a viable alternative to China's BRI.

The document noted that there was "still vast and untapped potential between Asia and Africa which needs to be explored [in order to achieve] shared growth, development, peace, prosperity and stability across this far-flung region." This could be realised by means of an "Asia–Africa Growth Corridor," it suggested. "The AAGC can become a sea corridor linking Africa with India and other countries of South-East Asia and Oceania by reviving ancient sea-routes and creating new corridors to link ports in Gujarat, India, with Djibouti in the Gulf of Aden [while] the African ports of Mombasa and Zanzibar will be connected to Indian ports near Madurai, and Kolkata in India will be linked to Sittwe port in Myanmar." The document then went on to suggest that "since time immemorial, the Indian Ocean linking the two continents has been a major source of closer trade, cultural linkages and people to people partnerships between Asia and Africa." This partnership, it claimed, "is ready for a big step forward as an economically virile Asia joins forces with an African continent whose economy is about to take a great leap forward."

For all the appeal to historical connections, there are hard realities behind the present battle among the US, Japan, China, and India (plus Oceanian countries such as Australia) to gain control over marine infrastructure. Access to Middle Eastern and other ports is essential to the United States both for economic and strategic reasons. It is equally important for China, which is now the world's second biggest economy after the US and a rising military power. China has been moving aggressively in recent years to acquire a string (or "necklace") of key ports around the world under its BRI. It doubled port investment in the year 2017 alone.

As one former Japanese government official observed to the author, ports have military as well as economic value and the AAGC provides a cover for Washington to gain access to maritime facilities in the same way that the BRI facilitates access for China. An example is the China–Pakistan Economic Corridor, in the name of which China has built a seaport in the Pakistani town of Gwadar giving China commercial access to the Arabian Sea along, some have suggested, with the power to mount naval blockades in extreme situations. From the start, the AAGC was regarded by many as a "copy" of China's BRI, but it was also seen as a "late-starter" and one that lacked the financial resources that China was pumping into the BRI. In light of this, Japan's Prime Minister Abe lobbied hard with the Trump administration to get the US and others involved in a wider design, one that would provide a credible alternative to the Chinese initiative.

Abe was anxious too to get Washington fully involved in Asia again following Trump's abrupt withdrawal of the US from the Trans-Pacific Partnership (TPP), an international trade and investment agreement that would have given the US and Japan together a decisive say in the formulation of regional policy. By withdrawing from the TPP, Trump had reversed his predecessor Barrack Obama's earlier "pivot toward Asia." Abe reasoned that even if Trump could not easily be lured back into an Asian regional trade agreement (given his preference for bilateral deals), he might be persuaded to enter an AAGC-like arrangement that could thwart China's attempts to gain strategic advantage in Asia.

The tactic eventually paid off and Trump embarked upon a swing through Asia toward the end of 2017. On a visit to five East Asian countries, he repeatedly referred to the region as the "Indo Pacific" rather than the "Asia Pacific." This was widely seen as a snub to China's ambitions to become a fulcrum power in Asia; at the same time it shifted the locus of the US–China rivalry from the Pacific to the Indian Ocean. Trump, however, did not come down specifically in favour of the AAGC plan during his Asia swing. The reason as it turned out later was that he had bigger fish to fry. He needed to wait until his administration could formulate its own response.

This subsequently emerged in the shape of a counter-strategy outlined in July 2018 when US Secretary of State, Mike Pompeo presented what he called an "Indo-Pacific Economic Vision." Pompeo announced that the US was ready to go into partnership with Japan, Australia, Indonesia, and others in building infrastructure across the Indo-Pacific region. Pompeo emphasised that this infrastructure would be built by private enterprise and not by Chinese-style state enterprises, another snub to China.

The Trilateral Partnership finally took shape during the November 2018 meeting of the Asia-Pacific Economic Cooperation forum in Papua New Guinea. Washington announced there that the US, along with its allies, "seeks to be a force-multiplier in the Indo-Pacific, providing a new vehicle through which countries in the region can coordinate their infrastructure priorities." While addressing the gathering, US Vice President Mike Pence brought the conflict aspects of infrastructure to more sharply into focus than anyone else had done up to that point. He described China's BRI as a "constricting Belt" and a "one-way Road," implying that Chinese loans come with strings attached and that BRI projects are designed principally to benefit China. "We are making infrastructure in the Indo-Pacific a top priority," Pence declared, "from roads to railways, ports to pipelines, airports to data-lines. The United States has a principled approach that stands in stark contrast to some other nations." This, he suggested, adds up to "a substantial new commitment from Australia, Japan, and the United States to the economic development of the Indo-Pacific through principles-based, sustainable investment in infrastructure."

While countering Chinese initiatives in Asia, the Trump administration is also presenting itself as a friendly presence in the region. "Our history in the Indo-Pacific," Pence argued during the APEC meeting, "is a story of trade and commerce, starting more than two centuries ago. Throughout our history, it has been a story of friendship and partnership, of bonds built over time with every nation — East, North, West, and South." The US relationship with Asia, he added, had always been "all about trade and commerce." These claims were rather undercut, however, at the same gathering by China's president Xi Jinping's observation that China's relations with Asia stretch back over more than "two thousand years."

Behind these competing appeals to history, the reality is that China and the US (backed in the latter case by Japan and India) are seeking to build infrastructure across the world's most populous and prosperous region in order to largely secure their own national advantage. For all the talk of historical commitment, the competing powers are intent on maintaining access to commercially and strategically important sea lanes. And, for all the talk also of standards and principles, the infrastructure contest in the Asia Pacific or "Indo Pacific" region could all come down to a dollars and cents bidding war.

Money talks and the US and Japan appear finally to have taken on board the fact that China is able to combine the resources of its huge state sector with private funds to be raised in international capital markets. The infrastructure challenge is not about millions or even billions of dollars, it is about hundreds of billions or even "trillions" of dollars. This will require funding vastly in excess of what governments and the private sector are currently providing. Having woken up to this fact, the US-led Trilateral Partnership has signed a Memorandum of Understanding (MoU) through which the partners hope to mobilise private investment in infrastructure (as well as in energy and digital connectivity) across Asia.

Pence noted that the Trilateral Partnership will have behind it the resources of the US Overseas Private Investment Corporation, which have been doubled to US$60 billion and those of the semi-state Japan Bank for International Cooperation whose balance sheet is comparable to that of the World Bank as well as funds from Australia's Department of Foreign Affairs and Trade and its Export Finance and Insurance Corporation. Yet, despite all this, the combined official resources of the US, Japan, and Australia available for overseas development projects do not match those that China can muster from its US$3 trillion foreign exchange reserves.

Despite the US bid to regain the initiative in Asian infrastructural development, the elements of the AAGC worked out primarily by Japan and India are likely to remain the basis of any rival to China's BRI. The AAGC at least has a conceptual structure for cooperation that does not exist within the Trilateral Partnership, at least not yet. It is possible even to see the trilateral initiative as an attempt to push China into a kind of "Star Wars" confrontation of the kind created by former US President Ronald Reagan in the 1990s to provoke the then Soviet Union into defence spending on a scale it could not sustain.

The idea of an "Indo-Pacific" alliance is not new to Japan. As far back as 2007 (as observed by the Japan-based Economic Research

Institute for Northeast Asia), Japan proposed the creation of an "Arc of Freedom and Prosperity" based on countries sharing Japan's fundamental values. This was similar to what later became Chinese leader Xi Jinping's "Silk Road vision" and eventually the BRI. Japan's original "arc" extended from Europe and Central Asia to East Asia, the Indian sub-continent, and beyond, but this was later scaled down somewhat.

The declaration by Japan's Prime Minister Abe and Indian Prime Minister Modi in 2016 envisaged several "pillars" of cooperation between the two countries with the ambitious aim of integrating Africa with India, South Asia, Southeast Asia, East Asia, and Oceania via the Middle East. This cooperation (as envisaged in the AAGC plan) is about far more than simply creating transport linkages. It is supposed to be "instrumental in creating new production channels, deepening existing industrial value chains, ensuring economic and technical cooperation, facilitating the flow of peoples between Asia and Africa, and achieving sustainable long-term growth." In order to avoid charges, such as those levied against China's Belt and Road scheme that it is more of a Chinese grand design than a cooperative exercise, Japan and India agreed on the need for wide and detailed discussions on the shape of the AAGC.

Few details were revealed, however, of how the AAGC was supposed to be funded and managed. It was clear from the outset that Japan would need to play a dominant role. As Masuhiro Kawai, a former senior Japanese government official and head of regional integration at the Asian Development Bank noted to the author, if Japan is going to play a major role, then "designing and financing by institutions such as the Japan International Cooperation Agency and the Japan Bank for International Cooperation together with local authorities and involving also private sector funding, would be a natural option."

At one time, the Asian Development Bank might have been seen as a natural agent to coordinate the AAGC initiative, in the same way that it has been closely involved in the Lower Mekong infrastructure development scheme among a number of Indo-China nations and in the Central Asia Regional Economic Cooperation or CAREC forum in Central Asia. But as Kawai observed, this may no longer be acceptable in terms of regional politics and diplomacy in Asia. The Asian Infrastructure Investment Bank has emphasised that it will not become an instrument for financing China's Belt and Road scheme and likewise Japan will need "to avoid using the ADB and the World Bank for building the AAGC," Kawai suggests.

While the AAGC has been slow to get off the ground, and the US Trilateral Partnership is still more a concept than a reality, China's BRI is meanwhile attracting strong support among Middle Eastern countries. China's "promise of an enormous infrastructure and investment programme [via the BRI] is understandably appealing for many MENA (Middle East and North Africa) countries," according to a study by the Washington-based Middle East Institute. "China is also expanding cultural and educational exchanges, promoting a people-to-people dialogue, as well as offering to train technical experts from BRI member countries." It is therefore "not surprising that many MENA countries are embracing China's vision."

Neither Japan nor India is likely, however, to cede victory easily to China in Asia's infrastructure wars. As the AAGC Vision Study noted, "Africa has tremendous scope for growth and requires development partners to achieve it." India and Japan "bring a shared repertoire of development cooperation strengths for Africa." India, it noted, has a long history of development cooperation in Africa in capacity-building and contributing towards development of a social sector through several unique programmes like the Pan Africa e-Network project. Indian companies have sustainable presence in the African region.

The AAGC Vision document nevertheless acknowledged that India's development partnerships in Africa are confronting "challenges of resource constraints" (RIS; ERIA; IDE-JETRO, 2017). It argued, however, that "Japan can play a major role to overcome these challenges." Japan has strong development assistance programmes in many developing countries, including the countries in Africa. Japan has expertise in designing, planning, and delivering infrastructure. It enjoys a leading edge in research and development. It also has the capacity to transfer capabilities for managing and strengthening supply chains in manufacturing sector and infrastructure projects.

China too has become an important economic presence in Africa, not least in the area of infrastructure building. According to the Chinese Ministry of Commerce, in 2000 trade between China and Africa was US$10 billion annually but by 2017 the value had reached US$170 billion. Chinese government financial investments in Africa have expanded hugely from US$5 billion in 2006 to US$60 billion. Bridges, dams, highways, power plants, and railway lines figure large among projects that have been financed by China in Africa.

China rejects suggestions that its investment in Africa represents a new form of resource exploitation or even "colonialism." It argues that it needs resources because it is a world leader in manufacturing and a major supplier for the global market. Economic cooperation between Africa and China brings mutual benefit and gains, not least in the form of modern infrastructure for Africa and employment creation on the continent. China's investment in infrastructural development in Africa comes with no political strings attached, Premier Li Keqiang has claimed. He has said that China "will not follow the beaten track of colonialism of other countries or allow the re-emergence of colonialism in Africa."

In the Middle East too, China has built up a strong presence. The United Arab Emirates (as the Middle East Institute has noted) is a founding partner in the Asian Infrastructure Investment Bank and will serve as one of the main transport hubs for the BRI. China's largest shipping company, COSCO, has partnered with Abu Dhabi Ports to build new terminals to support the expected increased flow of commodities along the BRI routes. Egypt has coordinated its own domestic economic plans with China's priorities while Jordan and Saudi Arabia are following suit. Chinese companies have already pledged nearly US$20 billion in infrastructure financing and have been awarded contracts for building major portions of the new capital to be established east of Cairo.

The BRI appears to have a considerable head start on the Asia–Africa Growth Corridor, the Trilateral Partnerships, and other initiatives led by the US, Japan, and others. Against this, there has been significant "pushback" against the Chinese initiative in countries such as Malaysia which has cancelled an East–West rail link project which was to be built using Chinese financing. Ideally from an economic, financial, and logistical perspective, these different infrastructure initiatives would be coordinated by a common authority and operate under common standards. But the risk from a political and strategic perspective is that BRI, AAGC, and other projects could duplicate one another, or they could even stall under the impact of great power competition.

CHAPTER 6

THE 'GREAT GAME' REPLAYED — WITH HIGHER STAKES

China's launching of its Belt and Road Initiative (BRI) along with competitive responses in the shape of the Asia–Africa Growth Corridor (AAGC) proposed by Japan and India and the Trilateral Partnership among the United States, Japan, and Australia have provoked comparisons with the "Great Game" played out in the 19th century between the British and Russian empires for political and diplomatic influence in Central Asia. This time, however, the battle is a broader and more complex one. It is a struggle for control of key land and sea routes across half the world and also represents an East–West clash between different economic ideologies.

The confrontation was probably inevitable once China began to re-emerge as a major economic power, reasserting the commercial and maritime strength, which the country had displayed in past centuries. Unlike the former Great Game, this one is being played using not the "hard" power of military might but a sophisticated projection of diplomatic and financial "soft" power, although with tangible strategic and economic objectives in view. China's entry into the new Great Game came at a time when Northeast Asia had long been seeking ways to transform itself from what former Asian Development Bank (ADB) Vice President Stanley Katz once called the "last major economic frontier" in Asia into a new economic power centre. Like Central Asia, Northeast Asia (defined to include Northeast China, North and South Korea, Mongolia, and the Russian Far East and even parts of Eastern Japan) has long been neglected in terms of economic development compared with other parts of the Asian continent.

This is partly because of political differences that have divided the nations of Northeast Asia from one another making it possible for outside powers to divide and rule, and it helps explain why regional cooperation has been so difficult compared to that in Europe or Latin America. As Takao Fukuchi, a former professor at Japan's Kyoto University, observed in the 1990s, "only Northeast Asia lacks a clear picture for its development, and it is a big vacuum in development of the Pan-Pacific region." This remains as true today as it was then.

Yet, the rewards of regional integration in Northeast Asia are potentially huge. With its vast resources, it is a "natural economic territory," as Katz observed. The potential for regional integration and exploitation of resources has become even more appealing now that North and South Korea have begun tentative moves toward closer economic integration, with the prospect of direct links between the Korean peninsula and China and into Central Asia and Europe. Lack of port, railway, and highway systems has hindered Northeast Asia's ability to exploit its oil, natural gas, metallic minerals, timber, and other commodities and to develop a manufacturing base, while poor transport and other infrastructure have been barriers to the movement of people and the development of tourism.

Efforts to open up this so-called "last frontier" were pioneered by South Korea and by China's Tianjin Province some 30 years ago with plans to launch a Northeast Asian Development Bank and to bring international financial resources to bear on regional development. These early efforts were doomed to failure owing to a lack of international support along with regional political obstacles. Things changed, however, once China entered the game with its BRI and with the parallel launch of the Asian Infrastructure Investment Bank. Prospects for developing Northeast Asia and the entire Eurasian continent improved dramatically with potential consequences for the way in which global trade and commerce is conducted.

As Kent Calder, a widely recognized authority on Northeast Asia and Central Asia, observed to the author, "things are very different now" and a crucial factor has been China's ability to "build bridges to Europe." Moves are underway to forge links across the entire Eurasian continent. The first regular freight train service linking China's Chongqing municipality in the East across thousands of miles to Duisburg, Germany, in the West, a project capable of halving cargo shipment times compared with sea transportation, was formally launched in 2016. Japan and China have begun cooperating on sea and rail shipments of cargo from East Asia to Europe via China and Central Asia. Mass movement of goods from the Far East to Europe offers an alternative to traditional sea links running through the Middle East and the Suez Canal. As Calder and other experts point out, China's Belt and Road plan will develop infrastructure across a Eurasian continent that historically has not been integrated and has conspicuously lacked infrastructure. China has until now been linked to the outside world only across oceans, but the BRI capitalises on China's geographic centrality to begin developing land ties. Building transport links across Central Asian plains, mountains, and remote terrain is a daunting but not an insurmountable task.

Along routes such as the Khorgos crossing between China and Kazakhstan, traffic has "exploded." Calder foresees China and Europe (Germany especially) coming together across the vastness of

Central Asia to form a new industrial production complex. Some experts are of the view that China's policy with regard to the BRI has echoes of the Victorians who first linked up Britain, and then proceeded to promote railways over what was then the British Empire, creating a legacy that helped to forge nations and which still lives on (K. Calder, personal communication, 2018; Y. Xing, personal communication, 2017). China, says Calder, for example, has "a lot of cards in its hand by virtue of its centrality and its economic scale. This is a combination which we have never seen before. It is like Germany when it began to industrialise after the Franco-Prussian War, a powerful nation in the centre of a Continent that is large and is growing economically."

Others claim that the relatively small populations in Central Asia and other parts of the Eurasian continent will render a pan-continental economic strategy non-viable. Yet, this misses the point that it is the markets that exist at either end of the new Silk Road that matter as much as what lies in between. German production chains since the end of the Cold War have been moving through the Visegrad group (the Czech Republic, Poland, Hungary, and Slovakia) to the East while China's economic centre of gravity has been moving to the West. As a result, supply chains stretching right across the Eurasian continent are becoming a viable proposition — provided that connecting infrastructure is built. Meanwhile, Hong Kong and the City of London situated at either end of the China–Europe supply chains can act as financial centres to finance infrastructure building.

Such infrastructure is likely to be stupendously expensive, and the BRI has been estimated to cost anything between US$1 trillion and US$8 trillion (Hillman, 2018; OECD, 2018b). The huge gap between these figures appears to reflect varying assumptions about what will eventually be included in the BRI and how many countries or continents it will ultimately embrace. President and Chairman of the Asian Infrastructure Investment Bank Jin Liqun acknowledged in an interview with the author that "there do not seem to be geographical limits to the initiative." The BRI, he said, is aimed at more than achieving "connectivity" within the Eurasian continent. "It covers the entire world."

The broad contours of the BRI have been set out, but what has been achieved so far resembles more an incomplete jigsaw puzzle than a grand design. Just how the pieces will fit together — and indeed whether they will ever do so completely — is open to conjecture. Just as China has not announced an estimated total cost of the multiple components of the BRI, it has also not given a target date for completing the project. China is by no means the only player in the theatre of operations envisaged for the BRI. There is some overlap between what the BRI and its related bodies plan to do and what is already being done by other multilateral development banks, such as the Washington-based World Bank, the Manila-based Asian Development Bank, the London-based European Bank for Reconstruction and Development, and the Eurasian Development Bank based in Almaty, Kazakhstan. These different initiatives will need to be coordinated or integrated in some way and the question of who will do so remains an open one.

The World Bank, which largely withdrew from infrastructure lending to the public sector for a couple of decades or more from the 1980s onwards after neo-liberal economic policies came to dictate an emphasis on private sector initiatives in infrastructure, is likely to assume a more central role again. This is partly because the private sector has been unable to live up to earlier expectations of its willingness and ability to fund infrastructure on the scale required, but it also represents a response to China's emergence in recent times as a powerful player on the global infrastructure stage.

Africa was once known as the "Dark Continent" when much of it was unknown and few people wanted to go there. The same could be said of the Eurasian continent, where Central Asian Republics divide Asia from Europe with little global interest in the largely unknown interior. But change is coming, and with it a new industrial revolution could begin. Kent Calder, who is arguably one of the few visionaries to have perceived this fact in his book, *The New Continentalism* published by the Yale University Press in 2012, chronicled what Francis Fukuyama called "the rise of a new geopolitical configuration" or Eurasian landmass that is becoming increasingly integrated by trade and economic developments. Calder, Director of the Reischauer Centre for East Asian Studies at the School for Advanced International Studies at Johns Hopkins University in the US and a former lecturer at Princeton University, sees China and Germany come together across the central Asian steppes and the Ural Mountains to form a major new industrial production complex served by extensive inter-modal transport networks and logistical systems. His book appeared a year before China's President Xi announced the BRI and China's vision of a "Silk Road Economic Belt" and a "21st Century Maritime Silk Road" serving North, Central, and South Asia and the regions beyond. The book also came ahead of Xi's announcement of China's plan to launch the Asian Infrastructure Investment Bank (AIIB), which has since come to fruition.

Relatively few people, says Calder, have yet grasped the full economic and geo-political significance of these bold initiatives. One reason for this, he suggests, is that South Korea-led efforts in past decades to launch a Northeast Asian Development Bank (NEADB) failed, owing to a lack of financial and other resources as well as the perceived competition with the ADB. As a result, the NEADB remained just an idea. Things are very different now, argues Calder, "China has been developing broader ties and a crucial element of the success of the AIIB has been the ability to build bridges to Europe. The fact that Britain was willing to join the AIIB along with other European powers is also decidedly important."

Technology is changing, particularly logistics technology, Calder points out. "The ability to do a substantial part of intermodal logistical operations between land, sea and air almost automatically and with low labour costs is making low-cost transportation across the [Eurasian] continent and development of logistical production chains viable." Some argue that relatively small populations in Central Asia could render a pan-continental economic strategy unviable, to which Calder responds, "space is becoming less and less of a constraint. The real 'core' to the likely success of the BRI and the AIIB is building infra-structure that will link Europe and China, particularly Germany and Eastern Europe. German production chains since the end of the Cold War have been moving to the Visegrad group (Czech Republic, Poland, Hungary and Slovakia) to the East while China's economic centre of gravity has been moving to the West."

The logic underlying the launch of the BRI and of the AIIB is strong. It is "there [Calder argues] in terms of the interdependence of European industrial production with China. German Chancellor Angela Merkel visited China eight or nine times after the BRI was announced." Calder notes "while Volkswagen has become a major motor vehicle producer in China along with BMW and other German vehicle makers and the two countries need to ship parts" to each other. Mannesman [a producer of heavy machinery], Siemens [a producer of electronics] and others also have a close relationship with China. "This will be a relationship of makers, manufacturer to manufacturer, facilitated by the Internet of Things and the revolution in logistics. Transport clearance has been rapidly improving across the Eurasian Continent, such that production chains are becoming increasingly economic." Germany's political relationship with China has evolved to become more cautious in nature in recent times because of Beijing's perceived possible economic and strategic threat in Europe but the industrial logic of the preferred Sino-German and Sino-European relations remains strong.

Constructing transport linkages across Central Asia's vast plains, high mountains, and otherwise difficult terrain sounds daunting, but this is not an insurmountable barrier, argues Calder. "Along the northern routes, for example, the Khorgos crossing point between China and Kazakhstan has exploded in scale in the last decade, particularly the past five years. There is a path between the two countries." The passageways between India and China are much, much more difficult, through Nepal and otherwise. Or between China and Pakistan — the Friendship Highway. They are trickier, but the passageways between China and Kazakhstan are largely flat — a plateau you could say. The geography is such that there are several routes that are viable economically if there is infrastructure, and that's where the AIIB comes in.

"It is important to remember," adds Calder, "that we are in the era of inter-modal transport so, this is not simply a matter of land. The AIIB and One Belt-One Road Initiative (OBOR) is also doing airports and ports. New road links become a challenge to historical ports along the long red line across Suez to India and to Singapore and Hong Kong. The Chinese are also developing the port side. They are playing it both ways." The BRI is huge and likely to be very costly, so how it is going to be financed? "This is exactly why I think the concept of a multilateral institution, the AIIB, is a brilliant development from the Chinese point of view. Huge sums are needed [for] Asian infrastructure and so it does need to be a multilateral, global effort."

The logic of China-led development of the Eurasian continent really became apparent after the 2008 Lehman Shock. "There has (as Calder notes) been a sea change in logistical economic relations across the continent since then." The surge of Chinese domestic growth in a period when the world economy was in contraction was a key force, Calder suggests. It began to get concepts and plans moving and that has continued even though the Chinese economy has not been doing as well in the last couple of years. I think in the overall scheme of things, the centrality and economic prospects of China, and the way that the AIIB capitalises on these, is a highly dynamic factor. We are no longer in the classical world of the "Great Game". China has a lot of cards in its hand by virtue of its centrality and its economic scale. This is a combination which we have never seen before — a country so central that it is growing so fast.

"It is like Germany as it began to industrialise after the Franco-Prussian War — a powerful nation in the centre of a Continent that is large and is growing economically." This has implications for US president-elect Donald Trump's policies. A US–Russia strategy will not suffice. Balancing China with Russia is betting on a losing horse. "This is equally true for Japan," he says. Tokyo is looking to cooperate with Moscow on developing the mineral resources and other resources of the Russian Far East. But this is a "sideshow" to what is happening in the more central parts of the Eurasian continent. "The logic of AIIB is basically building the infrastructural link between China and Europe, and that does not really relate to the Russian Far East. The Western part of Russia stands to benefit from the deepening linkage between Europe and China. But that's the area of the Urals into the West. It's not Vladivostok or Sakhalin."

Where does all this development leave the ADB, which is stepping up its activities in Central Asia? "It leaves the ADB in better shape than it otherwise would have been, because it creates an alternative route for China, responds Calder. China does not need to try to take over the ADB to achieve its objectives and conversely, Japan — or the US for that matter — can continue to pursue their objectives through the ADB without a zero-sum struggle with China. The way I see it, [the ADB can focus on] the southern Silk Road

across Vietnam, Thailand, Myanmar, the Bay of Bengal to India —
between Southeast Asia and India — deepening those ties — and
then on into central Asia and to Europe." Interestingly now, the
changed situation in Iran is opening up prospects for infrastructural
routes across Iran. That would allow India also to become a player.

CHAPTER 7

THE INFRASTRUCTURE BILL —
AND WHO WILL PAY

Much of the world is "in denial" about infrastructure. At the level of governments, business corporations, and individuals, there is an unwillingness to confront the idea that the physical foundations of our society — transport, energy and communications infrastructure — are in danger of subsiding beneath us, undermining economic prosperity and economic growth in the process and risking disasters. Even those who recognise such dangers seem unable to grasp the fact that financial systems in market economies are not structured to provide money for infrastructure investment on the scale required. The money is "there," but it is in the wrong place or in the wrong hands for infrastructure investment. Fixing this problem is going to require fundamental re-thinking about the way in which savings are collected and channelled into investment.

Put simply, the problem is that while governments are the main providers of infrastructure finance, their chief source of funding is tax revenues and those revenues need to finance a host of services other than public works — from education and social welfare to defence and emergency services. Governments can borrow but there are constraints on their debt levels, and nowadays, there is often a strong ideological bias against public sector participation in infrastructure anyway. The corporate and financial sectors meanwhile are often unwilling or unable to shoulder the risks involved in infrastructure. Global savings are adequate to do the job but there is no suitable mechanism to channel these into infrastructure. Finally, the multilateral development banks that were purpose-built for the task are prevented (again largely by ideological bias) from meeting the challenge.

As the BlackRock investment group observed in a 2015 report, there are three main pillars of infrastructure funding: governments and other public authorities, bank loans, and capital markets. In the case of governments and banks, both "have reduced the amount of capital available to commit to infrastructure investments in recent years, though they remain important players." Public deficits, increased debt-to-GDP ratios, and increasing pressures on public pension funds have constrained government budgets despite the record low borrowing costs and banks mainly have short-term liabilities (deposits) and so are not ideally positioned to hold long-term assets (loans) on their books. Capital markets too have real inhibitions about investment in infrastructure.

Infrastructure is something everyone needs but few are happy to pay for. As with public health and education services, infrastructure hardware is a "public good" that most people find essential and yet few are willing to spend money on. Yet, if the global economy is to continue growing or to avoid sinking into stagnation — social unrest even — the infrastructure bill has to be paid. It will be a very big one. We are talking about trillions of dollars for new highways, railways, power plants, and communications networks and about the need (literally) to stop the rot in the ageing and decaying infrastructure in both advanced and many emerging economies.

The Organisation for Economic Cooperation and Development (OECD) has estimated that some US$70 trillion of investment in basic infrastructure will be needed by 2030 simply to maintain the current levels of global economic growth. This is close to the size of the entire world's annual output or GDP, and it is well in excess of what the world is spending at present on infrastructure. Such estimates are a little theoretical because they use economic "proxies" for demand and then calculate how much money would be needed to meet that demand. But few dispute the fact that spending demands are going to be huge if economic growth is not to stall and welfare to suffer.

Infrastructure is not something that excites popular interest, unless it is the sight of dramatic and fatal highway bridge collapses such as those witnessed in the US and in Italy in recent years. It is not something that most people think about too deeply — it is just "there" to be paid for by governments via tolls and utility charges. This popular indifference or benign neglect has long been storing up trouble for the future. The global economy has been growing by leaps and bounds in recent decades, linking vast amounts of new manufacturing production with massive new consumer markets around the world. Yet the logistical infrastructure that connects the two has not been keeping pace. This says nothing of the huge strain put on infrastructure services by the rapid accumulation of populations in cities and other urban centres around the world.

The consequent surge in the size of the global infrastructure bill has been paid for increasingly out of public debt. Fortunately, the blow has been softened by a decade of historically low interest rates around the world but that particular "party" may be over now that monetary policy is slowly normalising, and the infrastructure bill needs to be picked up elsewhere. This means either by higher taxes or by making bigger calls on national savings, either through market mechanisms or by means of official fiat.

Some estimates suggest that as much as US$100 trillion of spending could be required in the coming two or three decades, depending on whether infrastructure is defined to include transport, energy, and communications systems; water and sanitation; and sometimes other facilities such as hospitals and schools. The Global Infrastructure Hub

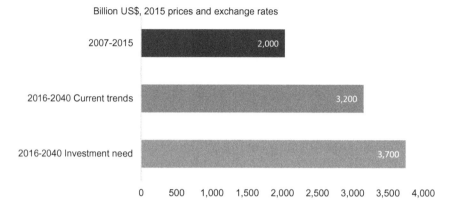

Figure 7.1.   Infrastructure — the Annual Gap.
Source: Oxford Economics (2017). Global Infrastructure Outlook. Oxford. Licensed from the Global Infrastructure Hub Ltd under a Creative Commons Attribution 3.0 Australia License.

(launched in 2014 by the Group of Twenty leading advanced and emerging economies to coordinate global infrastructure initiatives) estimates spending requirements between now and the year 2040 to be US$94 trillion. It has warned that as much as one-fifth of these needs will go unfunded if the current trends continue (see Fig. 7.1).

The estimated size of the "infrastructure gap" (between what is being spent currently and perceived future needs for financing) has been estimated by the McKinsey Global Institute (2016) at US$5.5 trillion in total between now and 2035, while the Global Infrastructure Hub has put the gap at US$15 trillion between now and 2040 (Oxford Economics, 2017), and this could rise significantly if infrastructure is to be designed to resist the ravages of climate change. The World Economic Forum suggests that the gap between what is now being spent on infrastructure and what is needed over the next decade or two amounts to around US$1 trillion a year (George, Kaldany, & Losavio, 2019).

Whichever estimate is used, the gap is likely to be very large unless more savings are directed into infrastructure. To achieve this will require a re-ordering of national priorities so that more of the income currently spent on personal consumption and on short-term "portfolio" investment goes to longer-term capital investment that raises productivity, economic growth, and incomes. However, this is unlikely to be achieved easily in market economies, and it will require new thinking about the respective roles of the public sector and of the private sector.

The building of highways, railroads, energy systems, and communications networks is obviously not something that is done at the personal level. It is done mainly in both advanced and emerging economies at the (central or local) government level in what are judged to be the interests of the community. Infrastructure is not always seen as being "owned" by the community, however, and taxes collected to finance it are often resented. Governments therefore find it politically more palatable to borrow rather than to tax in order to finance infrastructure. This in turn leads to a rise in public debt which limits further borrowing for financing new investment. As BlackRock has noted, "infrastructure projects lend themselves readily to government and other public funding sources as they often provide a public good" (Chavers, Synnott, Parkes, & Pilibossian, 2015). Yet, as a result, "public deficits increased debt to GDP ratios and pressures on public pension funds have constrained government budgets."

It is going to require acts of political courage and far-sightedness to alter the current situation. It is not that the money to finance infrastructure is not there but rather that it is not in the right place or the right hands to do the job. There are huge sums sitting in the corporate coffers and private investment institutions of market economies. These sums are available, in theory, for infrastructure investment, but they cannot easily be channelled into this critical area because suitable conduits do not exist in many countries.

The problem of making good deficits on infrastructure spending is most acute in market economies with their preference for consumption over investment. Data issued by sources including the US Census and Economic Information Centre, the US Bureau of Economic Analysis and the Federal Reserve Bank of St. Louis show that that ratio of personal consumption to GDP in the US has hovered at around 70 per cent over the past five years while data from the US Bureau of Economic Analysis shows that the ratio of personal savings to GDP in the US has declined from around 5 percent in 2015 to nearer to 2 per cent in 2020. Federal tax revenues meanwhile amount to only 18 per cent of GDP. In other advanced economies too, public spending on infrastructure lags far behind personal consumption. This reflects the triumph of short-termism over longer-term considerations.

The situation has persisted for decades in many advanced economies, largely because of a mistaken assumption that greater deployment of private savings in infrastructure investment was not necessary and that what was needed to attract savings directly into the sector was to get governments out. The reality is far more complex, as has become clear as infrastructure in advanced nations continues to decay while new facilities often do not get built.

Estimated financing needs for infrastructure meanwhile continue to soar (see Fig. 7.2). The McKinsey Global Institute (2016) estimates that the world will need to spend nearly US$70 trillion in

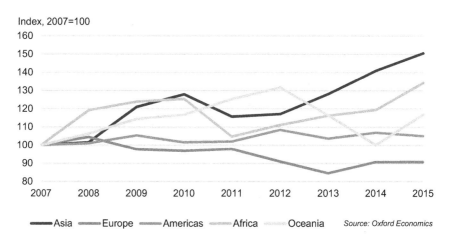

Figure 7.2.   Asia Leads the Way.
Source: Oxford Economics (2017). Global Infrastructure Outlook. Oxford. Licensed from the Global Infrastructure Hub Ltd. under a Creative Commons Attribution 3.0 Australia License.

the period from 2017 to 2035 on roads, railways, energy, water, tele-communications, ports, and airports. This is more than double the US$30 trillion spent in the 15 years from 2000 to 2015. The jump largely reflects the needs of key emerging economies for continued heavy investment in infrastructure. China, for example, needs to spend US$34 trillion and India US$8 trillion between now and 2035, according to McKinsey. In other emerging economies of Asia, Latin America, Africa, the Middle East, and Eastern Europe, spending needs are estimated at US$33 trillion.

These are big numbers and they reflect the fact that economic development and industrialisation of the kind that emerging economies are undergoing require huge amounts of investment in infrastructure. Manufacturing has become a globalised activity with production centres and "supply chains" often located far from the markets they serve, and thus needing modern infrastructure to connect them all together. This in turn demands complex cross-border networks linking together advanced and emerging economies.

Many advanced nations have neglected domestic infrastructure spending in recent decades. Having invested heavily in infrastructure in the past decades (or even past centuries if we go back to industrial revolutions in Europe and North America) and then again in the post-World World War II period, advanced nations have allowed their infrastructure to decay, to the point where it has become outdated and even dangerous in some cases.

Studies have suggested that the United States, for example, will need US$20 trillion of spending on infrastructure by 2035, Western Europe US$10 trillion, and advanced Asian economies (Japan, South Korea, Taiwan, Hong Kong, and Singapore) US$6 trillion (see Fig. 7.3) (McKinsey Global Institute, 2016; Oxford Economics, 2017). Views differ as to what constitutes "essential" infrastructure and what is "desirable." There is, however, broad consensus that much

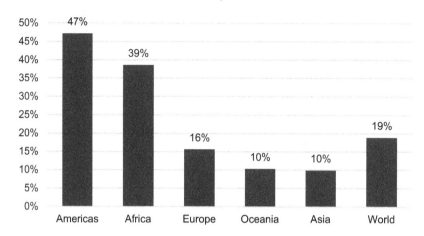

Figure 7.3.   America and Africa Fall Short.

Source: Oxford Economics (2017). Global Infrastructure Outlook. Oxford. Licensed from the Global Infrastructure Hub Ltd under a Creative Commons Attribution 3.0 Australia License.

more needs to be spent on building and maintaining infrastructure facilities than at present if economic growth is not to suffer and essential services not to fail.

This was vividly illustrated by two major (and fatal) highway bridge collapses (in Italy and in the United States) in recent years as a result of inadequate maintenance. The state of infrastructure in the United States has created alarm among policymakers and yet President Donald Trump is struggling to find even the US$1 trillion he needs for US infrastructure renewal. Similar situations apply in European and other advanced economies that pioneered public infrastructure provision but where now the inability to channel private savings into this critical economic sector has led to a funding drought.

It is a situation of "scarcity amid plenty." An estimated US$120 trillion is held by (chiefly Western) institutional investment firms such as pension funds and insurance companies. This is equal to nearly 40 times the current global annual spending on infrastructure and is also equivalent to one and a half times the size of global GDP. This money does not find its way into infrastructure investment on anything like the scale required. It is not only that the perceived risk in such investment is seen as being too great to attract private investment. There is also the problem of increased regulation in the international financial system since the 2008 Global Financial Crisis. This has led regulators to demand increased levels of liquidity at financial institutions and thus inhibited their ability to make long-term investments such as in infrastructure projects.

Many private investors have looked at the risk–reward ratio in infrastructure investment and decided they do not like it. No matter that investment in transport, energy, and communications facilities can bring financial returns over the longer term, short-term rewards are more attractive to portfolio fund managers and to bankers. The "lower-hanging fruit" appear more to the taste of private investors — be they banks, pension funds, insurance companies, or private equity funds. Restrictive covenants on the asset classes that institutional investors are allowed to buy are another problem, although infrastructure is becoming slowly more popular as an "alternative investment" or asset class.

The situation is of course different in state-directed economies such as China's where central and local governments finance 99% of the domestic infrastructure and the country has become a global leader in domestic infrastructure provision (Chen, Matzinger & Woetzel, 2013). In market economies, on the contrary, where the market is relied upon to arbitrate among competing demands for financial resources, the question of who should provide infrastructure has become a political football kicked back and forth from decade to decade between different players and conflicting ideologies.

Infrastructure is expensive and depending upon the type (whether local water or sanitation projects, mega-highways, high-speed rail systems, or power plants) can cost anything from thousands to millions or even billions of dollars and infrastructure projects, depending upon type, can take months or even years to complete. They are viewed as being fraught with risk — commercial risk that revenues from a particular service will not be adequate to cover costs; political risk (for example) that the rules of the game regarding service charges may change or even that projects could be nationalised; and financial risk of rising interest rates or other financial contingencies.

Unlike consumer or capital goods which are delivered in return for immediate payment, infrastructure projects generally begin to yield returns only after they are completed. What's more, revenue streams cannot be guaranteed over the long term even though infrastructure projects require huge amounts of up-front funding. Under such circumstances, private investment in infrastructure tends to be limited in quantity and selective as to quality.

As one group of researchers has observed, "private investment has contributed significantly to infrastructure development [but] it has been concentrated in less risky sub-sectors, reflecting a lower appetite for risk among private investors" (Gemson, Gautami, & Rajan, 2012). More high-risk areas such as water supply and electricity distribution meanwhile remain relatively neglected by the private sector and "recent projects in these areas indicate that the public sector together with the international financial institutions remains the main source of funding."

We are now in a kind of "no-man's land" where infrastructure provision and maintenance are often neglected and where everyone waits for the market to shoulder the burden while financial markets expect the state to ensure that risks are minimised. Market forces are supposed to direct capital to where it is most needed and to provide the most efficient way of managing resources. The idea that markets can be short-sighted in preferring short-term gain to long-term interest or that they can baulk at risk eludes those who argue for getting the government out of infrastructure.

Various methods have been adopted over time to meet the infrastructure financing challenge, with the relative roles of the public and private sectors varying according to the prevailing ideology. As the Asian Development Bank Institute in Tokyo has observed, "in the past, many daunting engineering works were successfully completed by relying upon imaginative and innovative approaches to attract private finance to projects for the greater public good" (Yoshino, Helble, & Abidhadjaev, 2018).

"In past centuries, privately owned railway companies in the United States and Japan serviced their massive debts primarily by selling or developing gifted real estate that was either adjacent to railway tracks or part of their rights of way." By the middle of the 19th century, "financiers knew that new railways could increase the value of land as much as four times its unserved value; for example, the price of land around the longest line in the world at that time, Illinois Central, appreciated from US$1.25 per acre to US$6.00 per acre in 1853 and to US$25.00 per acre upon line completion in 1856" (Yoshino, Helble, & Abidhadjaev, 2018).

The US Congress and the states readily provided inducements to investors "by granting public lands along the planned route to the private company that would build the railway. Far from costing the government anything, the granting of land meant that the alternate sections retained by the government would increase enormously in value as the railroads progressed and finally joined. Ancillary sources of neighbouring revenue were also relied upon, including mineral rights to coal and iron discovered on the land grants, which the construction companies could exploit for immediate profits.

"Together with city, county, and state governments directly investing in the stocks and bonds of private railway companies, the outright sale or mortgaging of gifted land formed one of the main sources of immediate revenue to service company bonds and pay its

bills before passengers and freight could be carried for fares"
(Yoshino, Helble, & Abidhadjaev, 2018).

In the 19th century, pioneers such as J.P. Morgan raised funds to
construct US rail networks (although governments were also
involved through land grants). The baton later passed to governments when private infrastructure came to be seen as a licence to
print money or as a source of monopoly rents. Governments of
Western nations became heavily involved again during the post-
World War II period of reconstruction in Europe. Yet the situation
reversed once again several decades later when private provision was
championed by neo-liberal economists who advocated an expanded
role for the private sector.

Then, during the 1980s and 1990s, the pendulum swung back
once more during the (British Prime Minister Margaret) Thatcher
and the (US President Ronald) Reagan privatisation era. At that
time, as the ADBI has put it, "governments became irrationally exuberant in their expectations of the private sector's ability to create
infrastructure out of thin air." Privatisation of infrastructure assets
was seen to be the answer, on the assumption that this would move
such assets out of the public sector and into the private sector where
they would be run more efficiently and profitably while governments would be relieved of a punishing burden of debt.

Once the "family silver" of electricity and other utilities had been
sold off (in Britain and elsewhere), however, private investors showed
less enthusiasm for financing new "greenfield" projects than they did
for exploiting the revenue potential of existing "brownfield" facilities
in area such as transportation and energy. As the OECD (2015) has
noted, the big jump in privatisation activity that occurred between
2009 and 2015 subsequently disappeared. Economies that had big
public–private partnership (PPP) programmes (such as Turkey,
India, and Brazil) then saw much lower activity. Compared to GDP,

infrastructure investment with private participation declined in 2016, to 0.3 per cent, its lowest level in 10 years.

The advent of PPP schemes from the 1980s onwards was greeted with enthusiasm by those who favour a bigger role for the private sector in providing infrastructure. Under PPP schemes, the private sector builds, operates, and maintains infrastructure services traditionally delivered by the government. However, as former President of the Asian Development Bank, Takehiko Nakao, observed to the author, PPP "is not a panacea" for infrastructure deficits. Or as Kevin DeGood (2014), Director of infrastructure policy at the Center for American Progress, has noted, "it is super-easy to mislead people that [PPP] schemes solve the investment gap." But they "are often [just] a way for a government to get money upfront in exchange for foregoing future revenue."

As Hiroshi Watanabe (personal communication, September 2019), a former head of the Japan Bank for International Cooperation or JBIC (a major global player in infrastructure) sees it, PPP schemes are distorting supply and demand for infrastructure. "Foreign investors in developing countries have become accustomed to demanding high returns on investment (typically around 15–16 per cent). In order to meet these demands, governments in developing nations prioritise big ticket items such as major highway or energy projects that are capable of yielding relatively high returns," Watanabe told the author. The real priority needs of such countries are often different — for water supply, waste treatment, and other essential services — but these are placed low down the list of PPP projects offered to outside investors, he said.

The peak year for private investment was in 2007 but after that the advent of the Global Financial Crisis sent private investment trends into reverse. Seven years later, in 2014, the OECD reported that "it is clear that the amounts available are still very limited compared to infrastructure funding needs and, at the end of 2012, they stood at only 11 per cent of total global infrastructure spending."

Private investment in infrastructure did subsequently recover but in 2017, the World Bank noted that, despite a relatively strong showing in private infrastructure investment during that year, "investment commitment levels still remained 15 percent below the average for the preceding five years" (World Bank, 2018). What this means is that while the private sector does finance roughly one half of infrastructure spending in advanced nations, this is a half of a much smaller pie nowadays relative to the size of the economies concerned — which is a recipe for infrastructural decay.

Now, the pendulum between public and private provision is poised half way in its swing as, on the one hand, China pursues state-funded provision of infrastructure at home and overseas while the US, Japan, and others gear up for privately funded infrastructure building in many parts of the world. The global context in which infrastructure is provided can best be described as being fragmented. Initiatives are often uncoordinated while financing is also fragmented as between public and private sectors of the economy, and the amounts provided often fall well short of what is needed.

There is no obvious way out of this "jungle," which arguably requires a fundamental re-thinking of how infrastructure should be financed and built, along with a new political consensus on the need for services, who should pay for them, how much, and by what means. The debate is becoming even more complicated now that cross-border transport, energy, and other infrastructure is being planned on an unprecedented scale via schemes such as China's Belt and Road Initiative linking Asia with Europe and rival schemes promoted by Japan and others.

It is clearly unrealistic to expect governments simply to "direct" more of their resources to building infrastructure in the way that, for example, China has. Fiscal and other resources currently available to governments are nowhere near large enough at present to meet the need, and in any case, other priorities such as social security spending (rising fast in ageing societies), health and education plus (regrettably) military expenditures, appear to rule out the significant additional spending on infrastructure.

Yet if, as the evidence suggests, infrastructure investment boosts economic growth and productivity, then the argument for augmented government spending seems compelling. The key is to shift public financing of infrastructure "off balance sheet" so far as national accounts are concerned and to find ways of directing savings into infrastructure by routes other than taxation. This will not be readily accepted in advanced economies where markets dictate the flow of private savings, but markets are manifestly not doing the job at present of funding infrastructure spending on anything like the scale required.

The concept of "national savings" needs to be revived, whereby governments or their agents collect savings for use in national projects. This has a certain "wartime" ring to it, but we are, as this book argues, involved in infrastructure wars right now. National savings can be collected through a variety of means including government-supported provident funds to which employers and employees contribute or from national or municipal bonds dedicated to infrastructure financing.

Not least among the challenges that infrastructure faces is the need to devise equitable financing models that do not overburden the current generation. As Amar Bhattacharya, former senior World Bank official, says, "a lot of the investments we are making today are actually investments for future generations. The big infrastructure projects that are being built now are for a hundred or even 200 years — in fact you could argue for millennia — because the backbone of such investments is a continuing investment in land, which becomes a very precious thing. Yet there is no reason why that should be paid for by today's users or today's taxpayers because tomorrow's users will be richer and more numerous than today's users.

"Before you begin to think about finance, a very important challenge in infrastructure is where are the revenues going to come from? There are two dimensions to this that are often not recognised. The first is the intertemporal one — that future generations should be bearing a lot of the costs and the second is what are known as "spillovers". These spillover revenues arise from economic activity generated along the route, for example, of new metro lines and the increased tax revenues this can generate through rising property valuations and business transactions. Riders on the metro system typically tap only into 20 per cent of the benefit from the system. The bulk of the benefit comes in the form of spillovers in economic activity [and increases in] property valuations in areas [adjacent to the metro project]. There is a lot of evidence now on these spillover effects that shows they are in fact tangible. When you take these two elements together, today's users should not be paying for future users. Today's users are tapping only a small proportion of the benefits of infrastructure projects. What is needed are funding models that can transform potential economic benefits into revenue streams rather than assuming that users are going to pay for the entire costs of a project over five, ten years or fifteen years. Once you are able to do that, you have a sound funding model which makes projects viable."

Infrastructure finance essentially needs to be "for the very long term" in order to match assets that are yielding returns over the long term with liabilities that likewise need to be paid down over the long term. Bhattacharya cites as an example the Washington D.C. Water Metropolitan Authority which made a 100-year investment and funded it through a 100-year bond. By contrast, developing countries and the major emerging economies lack sources of long-term finance, and the finance that they do have is of "very high cost." High-cost finance can turn viable, bankable infrastructure projects into a "non-viable and non-bankable," proposition, he argues. "By the time a project comes to fruition, the capital cost can be twice what it should have been. Finance is an enabler when it is provided for a long term, and at reasonable cost, and a killer when term is too short and the costs of capital are high. Most people are quite confused about these elements of finance. As a result, we have [supposed] panaceas: It is claimed that private sector finance can solve the problem when what is actually needed is a system of finance that is actually fit again for purpose."

Is such a model available? "I think so," says Bhattacharya. "We are now trying to change the discourse around infrastructure. I see the next five years as an extremely productive space for changing the discourse. A problem at present is that financing models for infrastructure projects are not well structured." It is a question, he says, of matching early-stage risk and long-term revenue-producing potential. "You need structures that are able to [take into account] early stage risks but without charging risk premia that are exorbitant. They need to be able to provide very long-term stable finance associated with the prospect of stable future revenue."

CHAPTER 8

WAYS TO BOOST RETURNS ON INFRASTRUCTURE INVESTMENT

A perennial problem with infrastructure financing is that projects (those involving road and rail transportation in particular) usually involve very large up-front expenditures running into many billions of dollars while the return on investment may often be insufficient to attract private investment, and even then, returns are typically spread out over a period of many years or even decades. Naoyuki Yoshino, former Dean of the Asian Development Bank Institute in Tokyo, is convinced that he has found a way to overcome this mismatch between risk and reward by capturing the hidden or "spillover" returns that transport infrastructure in particular can generate over time — and returning it to investors in order to raise returns and make infrastructure investment a more attractive proposition (personal communication, 2019).

Yoshino's ideas, formulated while he was an academic economist at a leading Japanese university, have impressed officials at the OECD in Paris and the Financial Stability Board in London where he has made presentations, and he expects to see them put into practice in a trial scheme in the Philippines before long. He explained them to the author during an interview in which he expressed confidence that the scheme could make infrastructure a more attractive "asset class" for investors. If a planned prototype scheme succeeds — and there are obvious questions relating to the collection, sharing, and administration of "spillover" tax revenues that are to be considered — it could be of interest to the financing of everything from China's Belt and Road Initiative (BRI) to Donald Trump's US$1 trillion plan to make American infrastructure great again.

The G20 group of advanced and emerging economies has recognised infrastructure as an asset class, and Japan, as host country of the G20 process in 2019, is working on ways to guide and regulate such investment. But this official blessing from the world's leading governments, while providing comfort to investors, will not of itself solve one of the fundamental problems confronting them — that of perceived inadequate returns on investment. To overcome this, infrastructure investors need to be given access not just to user charges but also to part of the indirect revenues that governments gain from infrastructure, Yoshino argues. "If infrastructure investment, such as rail or road transport, is built then new business will come to a region, business and residential areas can be developed and property values will go up," he notes.

Once infrastructure is built, "tax revenues from property will go up and corporate business taxes will go up — income tax and also sales tax." In the past, "these increased revenues all went to government and were not returned to infrastructure investors, who only relied on user charges. Especially with railways, prices are sometimes regulated by the government and also with electricity and water supply. So, there is a conflict between investors and users. That is why revenues are always very low. However, infrastructure can develop a region and then tax revenues will go up significantly."

Yoshino noted in a paper that, "it is well known that good infrastructure creates significant positive regional spillover effects around a project. Railways will bring manufacturing to the region by making the shipping of products faster, safer, and cheaper. Railways can connect manufacturers and farmers to markets and ports. New industry creates jobs in a region. Ultimately, service sector businesses such as restaurants and hotels are constructed to meet the increased business" (Yoshino & Abidhadjaev, 2016). Yoshino has proposed that governments — both central and local — should be required to return, say, 50 per cent of new tax revenues arising from economic development that results from the construction of new infrastructure to investors. It is possible to compute how much new revenue is generated by a project such as a highway or railway by comparing revenues in an area that has received such investment with those in another area where similar infrastructure investments have not been made, he argues. Technologically sophisticated monitoring, surveillance, and measurement systems make this plausible.

An official agency, such as the World Bank or (in the case of Asia) the Asian Development Bank, could be charged with overseeing and enforcing an agreement between the host (central or local) government on whose area infrastructure is built and the investor group of banks, insurance companies, and other types of institutional investors who provide finance, Yoshino suggests. Again, this does not solve the problem of low (actual or perceived) financial returns in the early years of an infrastructure project's operations, but Yoshino argues that this problem can be overcome with the aid of new financing approaches. Investors in a project could receive special infrastructure bonds issues by a multilateral development bank and the interest or "coupon" on these "floating rate" instruments would increase over time in line with the enhancement to tax revenues enjoyed by hosting governments. This could provide up-front capital to finance projects on terms attractive to the different investment groups involved.

"It has been estimated that returning part of the additional tax revenues from spillovers to construction companies and investors in the form of subsidies would raise the rate of return on infrastructure investments by 39–43 per cent in the case of Japan and by 14–16 per cent in the case of Uzbekistan (where the paper co-authored by Yoshino and others recorded experience with actual projects). A highway constructed in the Batangas province of the Philippines caused tax revenues to rise from 490 million pesos to 1.2 billion over a period of four years, according to an example cited by Yoshino.

Returns on infrastructure investment in developing and emerging economies have been declining overall in recent years. One reason for the decline since then is that governments in developing countries have started to run out of higher-yielding projects (such as major highways or energy ventures) that they could offer to overseas investors under the so-called Public Private Partnership or PPP schemes. In the past, they prioritised such projects knowing that they would attract outside investment but now they are having to give more emphasis to lower-yielding (although socially essential) projects such as those in water supply, drainage, and other areas.

"The rate of return in developing countries is going down because each hosting country realises the situation," a former head of the Japan Bank for International Cooperation (a major player in infrastructure financing, suggested to the author. "In the past ten years [host governments] put too much emphasis on PPP operations. At that time, each project was going to offer a high rate of return say 16 per cent. But in the past two years a discussion has started on how too much dependence on PPP is going to [influence] the priorities of each government."

An early form of infrastructure financing saw US state governments sell off agricultural land alongside early railroads, with the promise this held of capital gains for investors in the transport infrastructure. Other schemes (including in Hong Kong) have seen the sale of land adjacent to stations sold for its development and capital appreciation potential to help finance the cost of infrastructure development. But Yoshino claims that tapping the potential of future tax revenues to "subsidies" infrastructure investment is unique.

The approach based on collecting spillover taxes to sweeten infrastructure deals from the point of view of investors could have applicability to China's BRI (Yoshino, Hossain, Hendriyetty, & Lakhia, 2020). "Strategic, potentially game-changing projects like the [BRI] require vast amounts of infrastructure investment to be sustainable. Even in the absence of BRI, demand for such long-term investment is crucial to meeting the challenges associated with urbanisation, ageing populations and climate change." For Asia, demand will be greatest in the power sector, followed by transport telecommunications and water and sanitation, with East and Southeast Asia accounting for most of it.

"In many Asian developing countries, we observe heavy traffic congestion in cities, with highways, trains and various modes of public transport lacking. Public-Private Partnerships (PPPs) have been proposed for infrastructure development in India, Thailand and elsewhere. However, most PPP projects have been disappointing, since the rate of return on infrastructure [investment] depends mainly on user chares such as train fares and highway tolls. When the region was hit by economic crisis after the 2008 Lehman shock, the private sector withdrew from infrastructure investment" because the perceived risks were too high.

As Yoshino noted in a book (*Financing Infrastructure in Asia*, published by the ADBI in 2018) that he co-authored, "financing infrastructure is not a recent policy challenge." In the past, many daunting engineering works were successfully completed by relying upon imaginative and innovative private finance for the public good. In centuries past, privately owned railway companies in the United States and Japan serviced their massive debts primarily by selling or developing gifted real estate that was adjacent to the [rail] tracks on part of their rights of way.

"By the middle of the 19th century, financiers knew that new railways could increase the value of land by as much as four times. Ancillary sources of neighbouring revenue were also relied upon, including mineral rights to coal and iron ore discovered on the land grants" (Yoshino, Helble & Abidhadjaev, 2018). In Japan and elsewhere, permutations of the principle of using appreciation of land values and other gains to finance infrastructure have been applied, but Yoshino's scheme appears to be the first to use tax revenues linked to infrastructure projects to increase returns on such investment.

CHAPTER 9

INFRASTRUCTURE AND THE COST OF CORRUPTION

The global cost of infrastructure is destined to be huge in the coming years, amounting to scores of trillions of dollars, and adapting infrastructure designs to climate change could cost trillions more. But there is another huge and hidden "tax" on infrastructure costs in the shape of corruption. This again could add further trillions of dollars. Corruption in the way infrastructure contracts are awarded and administered is a major problem, not only in regions such as Africa and Latin America but also in parts of Asia. As U4, the web-based Anti-Corruption Resource Centre for development practitioners says, "corruption in the construction of public infrastructure has particularly serious implications for developing countries" (Wells, 2015).

Numerous initiatives have been launched at the national and international level to limit (if not yet eliminate) corrupt practices that are particularly prevalent in the global construction industry because of the large numbers of players — central and local governments, private sector construction companies, material suppliers, and others — involved and because of the huge sums of money involved in public project.

The Organisation for Economic Cooperation and Development (OECD) has been active in drawing up compliance codes and other instruments of international cooperation to fight corrupt practices. It notes that "governments around the globe seek to curb corruption to counter its negative effects on political stability, health and welfare, sustainable economic development, international trade and investment, and environmental protection" (Asian Development Bank, 2007). What the OECD calls the "keystone" to its efforts is the OECD Anti-Bribery Convention and the Convention's 2009 Anti-Bribery Recommendation.

The World Economic Forum (WEF), a non-governmental organisation based in Geneva, has been active meanwhile in highlighting the costs of corruption, which UN Secretary-General António Guterres suggested on International Anti-Corruption Day in December 2018 was costing the world a "staggering US$3.6 trillion in the form of bribes and stolen money every year" (United Nations Department of Public Information, 2018).

A few months later, a report by the WEF identified Somalia, Syria, and South Sudan along with the Yemen and North Korea as the world's most corrupt countries (while Denmark and New Zealand were declared the least corrupt) (Johnson, 2018). Other development experts add Nigeria to their "blacklist", while other countries such as Rwanda are said to be making sincere and fruitful efforts to address these problems. Corruption is a multi-faceted and almost ubiquitous phenomenon, however, and recent developments in the world of infrastructure have rendered that particular sector especially vulnerable to corruption on a large and international scale.

In 2016, China officially launched its Belt and Road Initiative or BRI (known initially as the One Belt-One Road or OBOR) to link

China with Europe via Central Asia by means of a massive network of road, rail, and maritime infrastructure channels extending also to the Middle East, North Africa, and beyond. This will involve more than 100 countries and massive amounts of spending for construction purposes. The BRI has spurred competitive schemes for huge joint infrastructure spending in much the same areas by the United States, Japan, and India among others.

Some of Japan's infrastructure competitors on the international stage (notably Japan and also the US and others) have repeatedly emphasized the need for "quality" infrastructure — strongly implying that theirs is of a higher quality than China's. They have not publicly pointed a finger at China as a source of corruption in infrastructure contracts, but one senior Japanese official with a long history in international infrastructure financing suggested to the author that Chinese officials tend to be "very loose" in this regard.

Around the time that China launched the BRI, the WEF issued a report dealing specifically with the problem of corruption in the construction sector (Matthews, 2016). This suggested that the value of global construction output was expected to increase by US$8 trillion to reach US$17.5 trillion per annum by 2030.

"It is difficult to determine precisely the value of losses through corruption, but estimates tend to range between 10 and 30 per cent," the report said. Experience suggests that "a similar amount could be lost through mismanagement and inefficiency. This means that by 2030, unless measures are introduced that effectively improve this situation, close to US$6 trillion could be lost annually through corruption, mismanagement, and inefficiency."

Losses on this scale "cannot be tolerated in any sector," the WEF suggested, and losses in infrastructure investment have particular significance. "This is because infrastructure underpins almost every aspect of economic growth and human development. It is a vital component of the most pressing global challenges we face, including eliminating poverty, achieving food security, rebuilding the global economy and dealing with the effects of climate change." Put simply, it added, "unless we rapidly improve the efficiency of infrastructure investments, our efforts to meet the great global challenges of our era are less likely to succeed."

The UK-based Global Infrastructure Anti-Corruption Centre (GIACC) has identified various features that make construction particularly prone to corruption. These include the fact that numerous approvals are required from the government in the form of licenses and permits at various stages of the delivery cycle, each one providing an opportunity for bribery. Also, investments in economic infrastructure such as dams, airports, and railways can cost tens of billions of dollars making it easier to conceal bribes and inflate claims.

The "uniqueness of infrastructure contracts is another factor which can contribute to the incidence of corruption," the GIACC suggested. For example, no two construction projects are the same, making comparisons difficult and providing opportunities to inflate costs and conceal bribes. Also, the delivery of infrastructure involves many professional disciplines, trade, and numerous contractual relationships that make control measures difficult to implement.

The situation with regard to infrastructure contracts is often more complex than appears at first sight, it was noted. Award of contracts is mainly based on the lowest bid, whereas evidence shows that lowest price bidding was more likely to result in time and cost overruns, leading ultimately to poor value for money and greater whole-life costs in the maintenance and operation of the built assets. A review of World Bank procurement procedures has resulted in a new procurement framework that "for the first time allows contracts to be awarded on criteria other than price."

Poor preparation of projects, whether due to corruption, negligence, or inadequate capacity, is particularly significant, as it increases opportunities for corruption later in the delivery cycle, the GIACC says. "When projects are poorly prepared, for example, when they are incompletely designed, are poorly budgeted, or have dubious or even non-existent benefits, it can lead to delays that may require changes that can be manipulated to benefit individuals or companies.

Now is the time, the organisation suggests, "to increase investment in infrastructure, but increases in public investment must be accompanied by reforms aimed at ensuring better value for money. This is primarily a challenge for government, but it is not one that it can meet alone. Companies can help, for example, by maintaining high ethical standards in their own operations and by encouraging their public sector clients to focus on improving governance and efficiency. Civil society can help too, for example, by acting as 'infomediaries' to interpret data on public investment for stakeholders and by supporting their efforts to act on it. There are a growing number of examples of the efforts of government, industry, and civil society being combined in multi-stakeholder initiatives or MSIs aimed at tackling complex governance challenges."

As the WEF has observed, however, "concerted action of this type has the potential to bring about a step-change in the efficiency of public investment only where is sufficient commitment across the institutional spectrum and for now at least, this type of collective action remains exceptional."

The OECD too (whose aim is to fight bribery in international business in order to strengthen development, reduce poverty, and bolster confidence) notes that "traditional approaches based on the creation of more rules, stricter compliance, and tougher enforcement have been of limited effectiveness. A strategic and sustainable response to corruption is public integrity" ("Anti-corruption", n.d.). "Such integrity," it says, "is one of the key pillars of political, economic and social structures and thus essential to the economic and social well-being and prosperity of individuals and societies as a whole."

Ten years ago, a number of governments in the Asia-Pacific region agreed to cooperate in the fight against corruption by launching the Anti-Corruption Initiative for Asia and the Pacific — a regional forum for supporting national and multilateral efforts to reduce corruption. Member governments formulate the initiative's strategies and implement programs and activities with the help of a Secretariat jointly managed by the Asian Development Bank and the OECD.

This initiative was originally based on the Anti-Corruption Action Plan for Asia and the Pacific endorsed by the member countries, which sets out goals and standards for sustainable safeguards against corruption in the region. Since the initiative's inception, however, international anti-corruption standards have advanced significantly, especially with the advent of the UN Convention against Corruption (UNCAC). In 2010, the initiative adopted Strategic Principles that guide the initiative's future activities and strategic direction and made UNCAC implementation a priority for the initiative.

Some 30 countries and jurisdictions from Asia and the Pacific have joined the initiative: Afghanistan, Australia, Bangladesh, Bhutan, Cambodia, China, Cook Islands, Fiji, Hong Kong, India, Indonesia, Japan, Kazakhstan, South Korea, the Kyrgyz Republic, Macao, China, Malaysia, Mongolia, Nepal, Pakistan, Republic of Palau, Papua New Guinea, Philippines, Samoa, Singapore, Solomon Islands, Sri Lanka, Thailand, Timor-Leste, Vanuatu, and Vietnam.

Membership in the initiative is open to any economy in Asia and the Pacific that recognizes the need for action against corruption and the benefits of sharing knowledge and experience across borders. It is said to be "actively taking steps to implement anti-corruption measures; commit to undertake reforms to implement the initiative's "strategic principles" and to participate in the review mechanisms" (United Nations Office on Drugs and Crime, 2004).

The initiative seeks to achieve its main goal of effective UNCAC implementation in Asia and the Pacific through capacity building based on peer-learning, mutual support, and exchange of expertise, while taking into account: the geographical and developmental diversity of its members; demands on members' human and financial resources; and the need to provide value-added in view of the functions and roles of the other multilateral anti-corruption bodies.

The initiative has built partnerships with the private sector, civil society, donors, and regional and international organizations. An Advisory Group serves as a forum to coordinate their efforts in support of the governments of the region. The group brings together the initiative's donors, the Ministry of Foreign Affairs of Japan, and the Deutsche Gesellschaft für Internationale Zusammenarbeit (GIZ) of Germany. Other members include international bodies actively involved in fighting corruption in the region: American Bar Association/Rule of Law Initiative, Transparency International, United Nations Development Programme (UNDP), and the World Bank. The initiative also works in close partnership with the OECD Working Group on Bribery in International Business Transactions and other OECD bodies, the United Nations Office on Drugs and Crime, and the other regional organizations.

As one Japanese government development expert notes, Asia is "not one hundred per cent clean" when it comes to the issue of corrupt practices associated with infrastructure, but the region is, he says, "much better than Africa and Latin America" in this regard. This same official suggests that "in the case of Africa over 10 per cent or even 20 per cent of GDP is kept by very corrupted people" (personal communication with author).

A notable example of a corruption in scandal in America is that of Brazil's Odebrecht. According to a 2016 paper produced by the Basel Institute on Governance, an Associated Institute of the University of Basel, Odebrecht was considered the biggest construction and engineering company in Latin America and a global leader in terms of infrastructure. Their work included roads in Mexico, a water purification plant in Argentina, a hydroelectric plant in Peru, and railways in Colombia among other projects. When the corruption scandal erupted, its consequences affected activity and foreign investment in infrastructure projects in the region at all levels.

It began as a money-laundering investigation involving a Brazilian state-controlled oil company, Petrobras, and developed into a fraud and corruption investigation into company executives who allegedly were paid bribes in return for being awarded overpriced contracts with construction firms. The investigations involved nine major Brazilian construction firms, in more than 11 countries, bribes valuing higher than US$800 million, and more than 100 contracts that had possible earnings of more than US$3 billion. It represented the biggest corruption scandal in the history of Latin America.

As noted above, the sheer scale and reach of China's ambitious BRI has raised concern in some quarters about the potential it could have to spread corrupt practices in infrastructure across several continents. Initially at least, such corruption (if it exists) has received little attention. The spotlight of international attention as far as the Belt and Road scheme is concerned has been turned mainly on what is alleged by some to be China's "debt trap diplomacy," whereby China is said to extend excessive amounts of credit to poorer countries in need of infrastructure in order to lure them into a situation whereby they are unable repay debts. China then demands asset collateral in the shape of land, real estate, or port facilities. China denies such charges, and some outside experts argue that if excess credit is granted by China for infrastructure facilities in developing countries, it is chiefly because of inadequate due diligence in project preparation of competition between Chinese state lenders to extend such credit.

The issue of whether or not corruption or bribery is involved in the award of projects related to the BRI has received little attention, although the senior Japanese official referred to earlier in this chapter suggested to the author that in his experience China would have little hesitation in paying bribes to an official from a recipient government where an infrastructure contract is worth over US$1 million. "In the case of China, they induce corruption in the other governments," the official suggested. "Even where China knows the government is corrupt, still they have no hesitation in supporting an operation. Northern European countries and the United States and Japan are very much stricter on these and we support good government, but I think China has no such principles. As long as they can keep some rights to resources or minerals, they don't care about corruption in other governments."

The Foreign Corrupt Practices Act in the United States is a federal law known primarily for two of its main provisions: one that addresses accounting transparency requirements under the Securities Exchange Act of 1934 and the other concerning bribery of foreign officials (United States Department of Justice, n.d.). The original Act was passed in 1977 and has been amended a number of times in the light of Congressional concerns that it could discourage US from investing overseas. Japan coordinates closely with the US on such issues and officials say that Japan is "very much obedient" to the US law as far as avoiding bribery of foreign officials is concerned.

Nevertheless, the OECD suggested in a report published in July 2019 that Japan must step up enforcement of its foreign bribery laws and strengthen the capacities of its law enforcement agencies to proactively detect, investigate, and prosecute foreign bribery offences. According to the report by an OECD Working Group on Bribery composed of 44 member countries, Japan continues to demonstrate a low level of anti-bribery enforcement (OECD, 2019). Since 1999, it has prosecuted only five foreign bribery cases and sanctioned 12 individuals and two companies. Japan's enforcement rate, the report added, is not commensurate with the size and export-oriented nature of its economy or the high-risk regions and sectors in which its companies operate.

As Amar Bhattacharya, a senior fellow at the Global Economy and Development Programme at the Brookings Institution in Washington, suggests, the next 20 years will be "more important for infrastructure development than at any time in history" because of the sheer size and scale of infrastructure networks that need to be created in this period and the efforts need to be stepped up to prevent corruption from becoming a major infrastructure "tax." This may not be easy given the reduced incentive for international cooperation under populist regimes, but without such efforts, the infrastructure financing gap may yawn wider.

CHAPTER 10

INFRASTRUCTURE IN THE SUSTAINABLE INVESTMENT UNIVERSE

Sustainable investment has graduated from being a "niche" concern to a central preoccupation among portfolio investors as environmental damage, social stresses, and governance failures (so-called ESG factors) exact an increasing toll on economies. Nowhere is there a greater need for investments to be made sustainable than in the area of infrastructure. Structures such as highways, railways, energy grids, communications networks, water supply, and sanitation systems need to be proofed against the ravages of climate change and they should wherever possible avoid social disruption and be shielded from corruption and poor governance risks.

Yet, such desirable ends come at a significant financial cost, which will be inflated sharply if infrastructure is to meet sustainability criteria. For example, the Asian Development Bank said in 2017 that infrastructure needs in developing Asia and the Pacific would exceed US$22.6 trillion through 2030, or US$1.5 trillion per year. This would rise to US$26 trillion or US$1.7 trillion per year if climate change adaptation costs are included.

Views differ on where the trade-off point lies between quality and affordability where infrastructure is concerned. Such differences of view are clear, for example, in the rivalry that has developed between China's Belt and Road Initiative (BRI) and the "quality infrastructure" approach of Japan and other nations (described elsewhere in this book).

Debate goes wider than these particular rivalries, however. It cuts to the question of whether returns on infrastructure investment are sufficient in the eyes of private investors not only to cover traditional political and commercial risks but also to accommodate the cost of proofing basic infrastructure against environmental and other risks. This is all the more important because infrastructure financing on the scale needed to compensate for deficiencies in advanced nations and to cover developmental needs in emerging economies cannot be supplied by the public sector alone. It will need very significant contributions from the private sector — running perhaps into trillions of dollars. As the Institute of International Finance (IIF) in Washington has noted, "there is a clear and urgent imperative to scale up and mainstream sustainable finance." And yet, as the IIF also observes, the allocations by private financial institutions to infrastructure assets "continue to be far below target" (Tiftik, Mahmood, & Poljak, 2020).

Huge sums of private finance are, in theory, available to help finance infrastructure building. The International Finance Corporation (2019) (an arm of the World Bank) estimates that as much as 10 per cent or US$28 trillion of total savings managed by financial institutions around the world could be attracted into impact investing — a form of investment that is well suited to infrastructure. Sums of this kind would be sufficient to enable the private sector to make a very significant contribution to achieving the United Nations (UN) Sustainable Development Goals or SDGs, thereby enabling the developing world to make major economic and social progress by the UN target date of 2030.

Among these 17 SDGs, only one refers specifically to infrastructure, but numerous others — including those relating to clean water and sanitation, affordable and clean energy, sustainable cities, economic growth, and climate action for instance — are dependent upon good basic infrastructure being provided. These are all areas — climate change impact alleviation especially — into which portfolio investors (socially and environmentally conscious "millennials" in particular) are showing increasing willingness to direct funds. The challenge, however, is to create sufficient investment vehicles to enable them to do so on a meaningful scale.

It is not possible to invest in the SDGs as such. They are concepts rather than entities. Official development institutions such as the World Bank Group and regional development banks among others can and do direct funds into sustainable development projects on a significant scale. But for private investors, whether institutions such as pension funds or life assurance companies or retail investors, access to goals such as sustainable investment in infrastructure is largely restricted to the individual company level. This means that such institutions are not able to invest "at scale."

The emergence of environmental, social and governance (ESG) investing has provided a conduit through which private savings can be channelled indirectly into infrastructure and other forms of sustainable investment. ESG provides a means and an incentive for investors and investee companies to incorporate social factors into their business decisions. Investors can influence corporate policies in support, for example, of sustainable infrastructure either by denying investment to those companies that do not conform to good ESG standards — or they can, by virtue of being active shareholders, exert influence more directly by means of encouraging good corporate behaviour.

The investment climate increasingly favours more intervention-ist behaviour by shareholders. Black Rock group chief executive Larry Fink made headlines in a 2019 statement to corporate CEOs by suggesting that society expects companies to serve a social pur-pose, and that it is their fiduciary duty to engage with asset managers on long-term corporate goals. Later, the American Business Round Table (2019), which speaks on behalf of 180 US chief executives, issued a mission statement urging Boards to substitute "stakeholder" primacy for shareholder primacy in the conduct of business.

ESG investing is gaining popularity quite rapidly but its size is partly a matter of definition. As the International Monetary Fund (IMF) noted in its 2019 Global Financial Stability Report, the "lack of consistent definitions makes it difficult to pinpoint the global asset size related to ESG, with estimates ranging from US$3 trillion (J.P. Morgan) to US$31 trillion (Global Sustainable Investment Alliance)."

The huge difference in these estimates partly reflects the fact that investors who favour the so-called "negative exclusionary" approaches often include investments in companies that avoid "bad" environmental and social policies as part of their ESG portfo-lio while others limit the designation to investment in firms that actively practice ESG. As David Semaya (personal communication, October 2019), executive chairman of Sumitomo Mitsui Trust Asset Management in Tokyo, puts it, "the challenge around the question of the environment as it affects asset managers and asset owners is, do we have a gradual engagement approach, or do we exclude com-panies right from the start. Our view is that we would like to proactively engage with companies to encourage a pathway going forward, rather than avoid investing because of perceived shortcom-ings in environmental and other corporate policies."

Another form of investment known as "impact investing" takes the ESG concept a stage further and requires a measurable social impact as well as a financial return on such investments. This is as yet a much more limited class of investment, and it is equal to little more than one per cent of the total ESG assets under management. The term sustainable investing meanwhile lends itself to many interpretations, and it has assumed a wide variety of forms, including "Sustainable Investing" or SI, "Responsible Investing" or RI, "Socially Responsible Investing" or SRI (often used interchangeably), as well as "thematic investing." Other classifications include "Green Investing" and "Social, Ethical and Religious" investing.

Despite the growth of these various forms of sustainable investment, there is a clear need for such investment to assume much larger dimensions if it is to make a significant contribution to the financing of "quality infrastructure" — let alone to the amounts needed under other UN SDGs and in more general applications. China's strength in promoting its intercontinental BRI derives largely from the availability of significant amounts of state finance, drawn from the country's official foreign exchange reserves and from state-owned financial institutions such as the Asian Infrastructure Investment Bank (AIIB) and from the Silk Road Fund and elsewhere among many state-owned institutions.

Governments in more marketised economies than China's cannot readily muster the financial resources needed to compete with China's BRI (as is explained in other chapters of this book). They need the help of the private sector and marshalling such assistance is not something that can be done easily among a highly diversified investment community.

The sustainable investment movement — whether seen through the lens of ESG investing and impact investing or through the prism of the UN SDGs — does however provide a possible means by which private finance can be encouraged on a scale required to have a significant impact on infrastructure development in advanced and emerging economies alike.

The need for such injections of private finance is not in question. As noted earlier in this book, expert estimates suggest that between 70 and 100 trillion dollars of spending on new basic infrastructure will be required globally by the year 2030, and the Asian Development Bank (2017) has suggested that one-quarter to one-third of this (US$26 trillion) will need to be spent in the Asia-Pacific region alone. The UN SDGs provide a channel through which private investment can flow into infrastructure alongside official investment. But as Vuk Jeremić, President of the Centre for International Relations and Sustainable Development and former President of the United Nations General Assembly, has noted, "too many key stakeholders still perceive the [UN SDG] agenda as being about governments coming together and acting in concert. Yet achieving the SDGs is a much more complicated undertaking involving not just states but multinational corporations, venture capitalists [and others]" (Partners Group, 2018).

Jeremić is not optimistic about the world's ability to achieve the SDGs unless efforts are stepped up with regard to infrastructure and in other areas. "I think we are under-achieving," he suggested in an interview with private equity firm Partners Group (2018). "As an international community, we are not doing very well. Our actions show that we have not prioritised implementation of the 2030 agenda. As things stand today, not a single nation is on track to fulfil the SDGs."

Marc-Andre Blanchard, a Permanent Representative of Canada to the UN and co-chair of the Group of Friends of SDGs in New York observes meanwhile that "though there will not be any one silver bullet that solves the SDG financing challenge, private capital is the one source both large enough and with the potential to reach the scale required by 2030" (Government of Canada, 2019). Total global financial assets, according to a paper by Blanchard (2019), have exceeded US$300 trillion since 2014. "Of particular interest," he says, "is the US$78 trillion share held by institutional investors with long-term liability structures and horizons, such as pension funds, life insurance funds, and sovereign wealth funds. Infrastructure investment, in particular, which represents the largest single component of the overall SDG financing gap, should be especially attractive to these investors because of its lower risk and stable real return profile which matches their real liabilities."

Not all investors are convinced, however, that the risk–return balance in infrastructure is as attractive as Blanchard suggests. This reservation applies not only in the case of portfolio investment institutions — such as pension funds which argue that fiduciary duty or sometimes statutory limits prevent them from increasing their exposure to infrastructure significantly — but also to "direct" investors who take stakes in the so-called Public–Private Partnership (PPP) projects with government entities. They cite, for example, the existence of political risks alongside commercial and currency risks in infrastructure. In addition, financial regulators are becoming increasingly concerned about the "liquidity risks" that investors such as pension funds and insurance companies can expose themselves to by substituting increasing amounts of "alternative" assets (such as infrastructure) for more liquid and short-term financial assets in their portfolios.

Such concerns are susceptible to being overridden or at least diluted, however, as the sustainable investment debate gains support among increasingly large sections of the investor community as well as the public at large. Investment decisions will likely reflect to an increasing extent the preferences of individual investors — whether they be investing through mass participation instruments such as Exchange Traded Funds (ETFs) or "millennials" controlling large sums of inherited wealth. With the dangers of climate change looming increasingly large, many of these investors are expected to require that their funds be directed into infrastructure and related areas than has been the case in the past.

Up to now, sustainable portfolio investment has overwhelmingly taken the form of equity securities, but fixed-income forms of sustainable investment are rapidly gaining popularity. ESG, which aims to steer corporate activity in sustainable directions, is the most widely practised form of sustainable investment. The so-called Impact Investing goes further and requires investments to have a measurable social impact. Critically, it also assures the investor of a financial return which means that social goals can be achieved along with fulfilling financial fiduciary obligations. This is particularly important for institutional investors, who generally are unable to sacrifice financial returns for wider social obligations.

The impact investing universe appears poised to expand dramatically from here on, however, as the UN seeks to fund its ambitious SDGs on the one hand and, on the other hand institutional and individual investors (as well as official development institutions) seek to secure measurable social impact in addition to financial returns on their investments. Because of its insistence on the need to achieve measurable social impact, impact investing is seen as being well suited to guide private savings into achieving social targets across a broad spectrum. This is vital if the UN targets are to be met as collectively they could require US\$2–3 trillion of private investment annually plus similar amounts of official funding (UNCTAD, 2014).

As the Global Impact Investing Network (GIIN) puts it, "Impact investing challenges the view that social and environmental issues should be addressed only by philanthropic donations and government aid and that market investments should focus exclusively on financial returns. It has the potential to reshape the role of capital in society, demonstrating that social and economic progress can be made alongside financial returns" (n.d.). According to the GIIN (n.d.), impact investments are investments made into companies, organizations, and funds with the intention to generate social and environmental impact alongside a financial return. Impact investments can be made in both emerging and developed markets and target a range of returns from below market to market rate, depending upon the circumstances.

Impact investors include fund managers, development finance institutions, diversified financial institutions and banks, private foundations, pension funds and insurance companies, family offices, and non-governmental organisations (NGOs) among others. Investments are not defined by their membership in an asset class, but by the approach of the investor. They may be made into the full range of public and private assets, as long as the investor contributes to achieving impact.

Impact investing and ESG can together be seen as part of a sustainable investment "revolution" which is essential if critical climate and environmental goals are to be achieved and threats to social instability avoided. The revolution will present not only huge challenges to global finances but also big opportunities for financial institutions to benefit from the changes involved. The impact investing market is still small relative to other forms of sustainable investment and is at around US$1 trillion according to the International Finance Corporation (IFC) (N. Gregory, personal communication, 2019). But the World Bank-related organisation believes that impact investing is set to grow dramatically in the coming years and that its size could grow to around one-tenth of the global financial assets or more than US$25 trillion over time.

All in all, it appears that the structure of financing in market economies — the shift to various forms of sustainable investment in particular — is evolving in ways that should assist the channelling of savings into infrastructure. This should help such economies to marshal funds on a scale approaching that in state-controlled economies. But the process will necessarily be an extended one because of the magnitude of the structural changes, which are required to be more imminent. This could mean that state initiatives become even more important in infrastructure financing, at least for a time, as the process of financial system evolution in market economies catches up with new realities.

CHAPTER 11

QUANTITY VERSUS QUALITY IN INFRASTRUCTURE

Part of the fallout from the current infrastructure wars is an acrimonious debate over the need for so-called quality infrastructure. This issue has aroused such strong emotions as to cause US Vice President Michael Pence to launch a fierce tirade against China; Japan to disparage China and other infrastructure rivals; the World Bank to join other development banks in veiled warnings about the dangers of inferior infrastructure; and the G20 nations to pronounce upon infrastructure quality in official communiqués.

But there are valid reasons for differing views on "quality" in infrastructure, as Hiroshi Watanabe, a former head of the Japan Bank for International Cooperation, a major player in infrastructure acknowledged in conversation with the author. It has to do partly with affordability and even with politics, he notes. Budgetary constraints often intrude on the choice of infrastructure, especially in the case of emerging and developing economies, while politicians in government can often be tempted to choose systems that will show results while they are still in office regardless of quality.

Infrastructure has become highly politicised since China embarked on building a vast domestic network of transport and other infrastructure

Figure 11.1. "Quality" Infrastructure — US Style.
Source: Brandi Jade Thomas/Pioneer Press. https://www.twincities.com/2017/07/29/the-day-a-bridge-collapsed-in-minneapolis-and-lives-changed-forever/

and then announced in 2013 a plan to connect itself with the rest of the world via the Belt and Road Initiative (BRI) (Ministry of Foreign Affairs of the People's Republic of China, 2013). This semi-global web of land and sea connections provoked concerns that China was seeking to become a global superpower via infrastructure, and in 2016, the G20 group of nations began stressing the need for "quality infrastructure" in what was

Figure 11.2. "Quality" Infrastructure — Italian Style.
Source: Luca Zennaro/ANSA via AP. https://s.abcnews.com/images/International/genoa-bridge-collapse3-ap-ml-180814_hpMain_16x9_992.jpg.

perceived to be a counter to China's infrastructure blitz (OECD; International Monetary Fund, 2019).

Moreover, attacks ensued on China's plans (such as claims that it was designed to lure host countries of Belt and Road projects into getting so deep into debt that they would lose control over strategic assets to China). But the implication that China-supplied infrastructure was something less than the "quality infrastructure" supplied by others appeared to have been designed to thwart the Chinese initiative. Some saw deep irony in all this. However, the "quality infrastructure" claim came at a sensitive time when certain Western nations had suffered a series of disasters from decaying public transport facilities.

A major highway bridge collapsed in Minnesota, USA, in 2009, followed in 2018 by a similar collapse of a bridge in Genoa, Italy. Both resulted in multiple deaths and injuries (see Figs. 11.1 and 11.2). Japan also suffered a road tunnel collapse (with injuries and fatalities) in 2012, and Germany witnessed a rail tunnel collapse in 2017. All this served to reveal the decrepit state of many highways and railroads in the US and elsewhere.

For advanced nations to be criticising China over infrastructure quality therefore seemed to be unjustified if not downright hypocritical. The term "quality infrastructure" has been applied in a very general sense, however, that goes beyond the inferior "steel and concrete" imagery that it conjures up. It has become a veiled criticism of the Chinese way of "doing business" with other developing and advanced nations.

Pence's outburst against China (although he did not mention the country by name) during the 2018 APEC summit was as much a sign of resentment by the world's biggest economy at China's global initiative on infrastructure as it was an attack on the quality of Chinese construction *per se*. He focussed on China's alleged "debt-trap diplomacy" in financing infrastructure and its lack of transparency, governance standards, and procurement methods.

China's launch in 2016 of the Asian Infrastructure Investment Bank (AIIB), which was specifically designated as an "infrastructure" financing institution rather than a general "development" bank, also provoked resentment and fear that Beijing would embark upon a global blitz of infrastructure building using its US$3 trillion foreign exchange reserves to finance it (Xi, 2016).

There were charges too that China would use the BRI (backed by the AIIB) to export surplus construction capacity and dump inferior quality infrastructure on the developing nations. All of this resentment became wrapped up in a kind of code phrase — "quality infrastructure" — to denote the supposed merits of Western (and Japanese) infrastructure versus the perceived vices of the Chinese approach. The term "quality infrastructure" then became subsumed within a wider policy debate. When the United Nations published its SDGs in 2015, infrastructure was included, with emphasis on the need to create environmentally friendly and sustainable facilities (United Nations, 2015a). Likewise, when the G20 group of advanced and emerging economies held its summit in China in 2016, there was pressure to include a reference to quality infrastructure (Ministry of Foreign Affairs of the People's Republic of China, 2016).

The leaders' communiqué announced a "commitment to pro-mote investment with focus on infrastructure, in terms of both quantity and quality. We stress the importance of quality infrastructure investment which aims to ensure economic efficiency in view of life-cycle cost, safety, resilience against natural disaster, job creation, capacity building and transfer of expertise, and know-how on mutually agreed terms and conditions" ("G20", 2016).

The fact that "life-cycle cost" headed the list was significant in view of Japan's insistence on its importance and its assertion that "Japanese quality" is superior to that of the rival Asian suppliers of infrastructure such as China and South Korea. This is not simply a question of Japan promoting its own interests. The quality infrastructure debate does have its positive aspects and some of these are stressed by Hiroshi Watanabe (personal communication, November 2019), a former head of the Japan Bank for International Cooperation, a major player in infrastructure.

As the chair country of the G20 (in 2019), Japan, he notes, promoted high-quality infrastructure. "Each host country is going to have to trade off cheaper against better. Many countries have a tendency to choose the cheaper but if you look at life cycle cost with the cheaper reliability is not so good. Five or ten years later you have to invest more money in the same project." Governments, Watanabe suggests, are often "rather short-sighted" with regard to infrastructure. National leaders are influenced by short-term political considerations and choose projects that can be completed quickly within their terms of office, and by choosing cheaper over more expensive infrastructure, they can complete more projects within a given budget.

"In many developing or emerging economies in the formulation of the budget, new construction will take priority while maintenance and repair are much neglected. We [Japan] are going to say that as far as you have biases in budget formation, you can [prioritise] new construction but neglecting repairs and maintenance can be costly." Choosing cheaper infrastructure can result in malfunctions after 7 or 8 years, requiring costly repairs, whereas Japanese projects typically function for 15 years. So, adds Watanabe, "either, make provision for repairs and maintenance or adopt better quality and more durable projects."

Nevertheless, Japan has seen competitors such as China and South Korea make major inroads into infrastructure construction markets in and beyond Asia that it once regarded as its home territory. It needs to work in conjunction with rather than in competition with such competitors in future. "In the past ten years our prices [for infrastructure projects] have been high," Watanabe acknowledges, "but now we are going to invite other countries to provide parts of [contributions to] construction. Our costs are much more expensive than [those of the] Chinese and a little more expensive than Korean."

Watanabe's comments appeared to shed light on the agreement in late 2018 between Japanese Prime Minister Shinzo Abe and Chinese President Xi Jinping that the two countries hoped to find ways to cooperate on joint infrastructure projects in third countries ("Abe, Xi Agree", 2018). Such cooperation appears unlikely to extend yet to full-fledged Japanese cooperation with China's BRI (or Japanese membership of the China-led Asian Infrastructure Investment Bank), but joint ventures overseas in which Japan has some input on the quality of the project could provide an interim *modus operandi* or *modus vivendi*. One senior Japanese Ministry of Finance official commented to the author that "there should be a spectrum of quality [in infrastructure]." Japanese quality "might be too much for small economies," he acknowledged, but added that when developing countries wish to graduate to middle-income status, "they need to tap the technology provided by Japanese companies."

Tokyo sees the G20 as a neutral vehicle for promoting "quality" where infrastructure is concerned (and Japan firmly believes that its name is synonymous with the idea of quality). With what Watanabe claims is now a "consensus" among the advanced and emerging economies of the G20 in favour of pursuing quality infrastructure, Japan's aim (according to its finance ministry) is to "go into these elements a little deeper and see if anything is missing [and to come up with a new set of principles and practices other than just language in the communiqué" (personal communication, November 2019). The G20 has recognised infrastructure as an "asset class" for investors, but there is an "information gap" to be closed before this can be achieved, Japanese officials argue. "Rather than push our ideas we will try to collect ideas from among the G20 countries" (H. Watanabe, personal communication, November 2019).

CHAPTER 12

MULTILATERAL DEVELOPMENT BANKS AND THE INFRASTRUCTURE GAP

If multilateral development banks (or MDBs as they are often known) did not exist, they would need to be invented. The fact is, of course, that they do exist, but they are not being used fully for one of the primary purposes they were designed for, and that is the provision of infrastructure. There are no fewer than 25 global, regional, or sub-regional MDBs throughout the world plus a couple of 100 smaller national development banks (Prizzon & Engen, 2018). The problem is that, despite being structured specifically as "banks" and not simply as development "agencies," these unique institutions are expected to deal with myriad issues ranging from health and welfare to education and environmental policies with dozens of other tasks thrown in. They have been relegated to the role of secondary players in infrastructure, whereas they were designed originally to act as principals.

As Britain's Overseas Development Institute (ODI) has noted, MDBs are "caught between a rock and a hard place" with increasing mandates and stagnating resources (Prizzon & Engen, 2018). Many of them were created in the 1960s during the period of decolonisation in order to promote economic development while others came into being after the end of the Cold War to support reconstruction and regional integration. The MDBs were later called upon to step up efforts in the pursuit of the UN Millennium Development Goals and now of the more ambitious Sustainable Development Goals. They are, as the ODI put it, "expected to" address a growing list of global challenges "such as climate change, mass migration and pandemics."

The fact that the MDBs are often overloaded with tasks for which they are not properly suited, and that they sometimes try to over-reach themselves, has often been commented upon. But what seems to have escaped wider attention is that the unique advantage MDBs possess as banking institutions — by virtue of having access to public and private financial resources — is being squandered while policy-makers vainly seek other means to finance infrastructure.

There is wide agreement on the existence of an "infrastructure gap" — the difference between what is being spent at present and what needs to be spent on transport, energy, communications, and other facilities both now and in the future. Estimates differ as to how big this gap is, but the MDBs themselves have estimated the gap between supply and demand for infrastructure funds at US$1 trillion a year at least in developing and emerging economies alone (Fuerer, 2015).

Governments have by tradition been the chief providers of infra-structure funds, but they cannot afford to close the funding gap by themselves because of their own financial and other constraints. Meanwhile private investors, even though they could in theory afford to plough billions or even trillions more dollars into infra-structure, hesitate to do so because of the perceived excessive risk this entails or because of what are regarded in the private sector as being inadequate returns on investment.

Policymakers in advanced economies have spent many years wrestling with the problem of how to lure more money held in private institutional and corporate savings into infrastructure when in fact the solution has been "hidden in plain sight." The reason for this is chiefly that an ideological bias has blinded many politicians, government officials, and economists to the unique characteristics that make MDBs ideal conduits for transferring resources into the critical area of infrastructure.

The presence of most of the world's leading governments among their shareholders allows the MDBs to obtain sovereign credit ratings that are higher than those of some of the governments themselves, as well as being above those of private sector institutions. This is reflected in the "Triple A" status which most of the MDBs enjoy when they issue debt instruments on international bond markets. That in turn enables the banks to on-lend funds (chiefly to governments but sometimes to private borrowers) at below-market rates of interest in order to finance infrastructure and other projects.

All this means that MDBs are better positioned to raise funds than individual governments or project and construction companies which do not enjoy the same status. A bond issued, for example, by the World Bank is backed by the credit standing of the bank's 189 shareholder governments, which in effect guarantee the debt. Institutional investors such as pension funds or insurance companies (even individual investors) can buy such bonds knowing that they are backed by an official entity. This is very important given that so many private sector investors are reluctant to invest directly in infrastructure. They require some sort of "comfort blanket" or guarantor before they lend — and that is exactly the role the MDBs are able to play.

The MDBs are cost-effective too in that only a small portion of the capital that shareholder governments pledge to them actually needs to be "paid in." The rest is "callable" at will and then only in case of emergency (see Fig. 12.1). And, unlike commercial banks

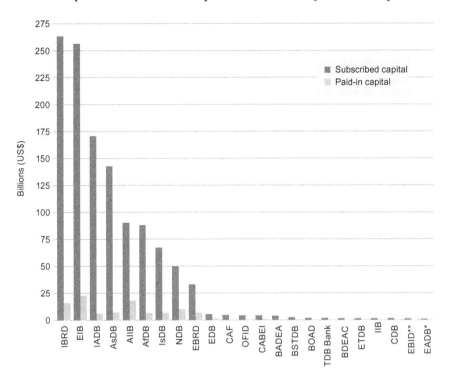

Figure 12.1.   MDBs Offer a Big Bang for their Buck.

Source: Prizzon, A. and Engen, L. (2018). *A Guide to Multilateral Development Banks.* London: Overseas Development Institute, p. 26.

whose deposits are of a short-to-medium-term nature, the MDBs issue long-term bonds so that their funds can be used to support long-term lending. As suggested, if the MDBs did not exist, they would need to be invented and it would be difficult to devise new institutions better suited to tackle the challenge of long-term lending for infrastructure. Yet, this fact seems to be almost wilfully ignored.

Only a few of the leading 25 multilateral development institutions (such as the Asian Infrastructure Investment Bank (AIIB), the East African Development Bank, and the New Development Bank or "BRICS" bank) have infrastructure development included in their specific mandate or articles of association. However, most of the MDBs are charged with the task of promoting economic development and regional economic cooperation. Infrastructure development is obviously a very important component of all of these missions — arguably the single most important one.

Given that these bridges for closing the "infrastructure gap" already exist, why are they not being made use of more effectively? It is true that their finances are not big enough at present (even in aggregate) to bridge the infrastructure gap entirely, but governments have only to subscribe limited amounts of extra capital to the development banks for their lending power to be leveraged greatly. The real reason, however, why MDBs are not being fully utilised for the purpose of infrastructure financing has as much to do with politics as it does with finance.

The situation in which MDBs find themselves is a microcosm of a wider ideological conflict between private and public enterprise. This limits the power of multilateral public institutions when it comes to their engagement with market economies. In their zeal to ensure that such public institutions do not "crowd out" private enterprise, advocates of a market approach to infrastructure financing tend to overlook the fact that often the private sector has little desire or ability to be "crowded in" in the first place. This is nowhere more true than when huge capital investments are required "up-front" in projects that yield financial returns only over the long term and which are often perceived to be fraught with commercial and political risk.

Another reason why the MDBs are not used in a more effective manner is that they have so many different agendas to accomplish. Politics is again a potent factor in this regard because national legislatures in countries that make up the shareholder base of the MDBs often demand policy inputs in return for subscriptions of capital. As Yuqing Xing, an economics professor at the National Graduate Centre for Policy Studies in Tokyo, observed to the author, some MDB's have been "captured" by government and non-governmental lobbies. These lobbies often, according to Xing, "do not examine cost-benefit analyses, only environmental factors in judging projects. They do not consider financial costs — yet someone has to pay."

These multiple demands made on MDB lending from shareholding countries have in turn caused the MDBs to impose tight lending "conditionality" on borrowers who have to promise the lending banks they will adhere to environmental, sociological, and other "safeguards" before they can hope to qualify for loans. Even then, loan approvals may take several years. Yet, as Masahiro Kawai, a former senior official at the Asian Development Bank, acknowledged to the author, developing countries "do not wish to see very tight (lending) safeguards." It is the governments of developed countries that want to see wide-ranging conditions imposed upon borrowers, because those governments need to answer to broad constituencies at home. As Kawai put it, non-governmental agencies and other civil society groups "can come at you and you don't want to be criticised."

The MDBs are often in no position to resist shareholder demands and sometimes they compound the problem by succumbing to empire building ambitions. One former British government development minister was prompted to remind the then president of the World Bank that there were "other aid agencies in the world in addition to the World Bank" as his desire for the bank to take on additional tasks appeared to expand infinitely (personal communication, n.d.). Another former World Bank president, a former medical doctor, acknowledged to the author that while his bank was not best equipped to says deal with health matters, as head of the World Bank, he enjoyed far more power to secure resources than if he were the head of another United Nations agency. Such examples illustrate the misuse of the MDB mission by shareholders and management alike.

It might appear from some perspectives that MDBs are in fact a significant force in financing infrastructure. Britain's ODI for one claims that, "infrastructure is the largest sector supported by [MDBs] reflecting their key mandates" (Prizzon & Engen, 2018). Among 25 leading development banks, one-half allocate more than 50 per cent of their loan disbursements to infrastructure — chiefly to transport projects, followed by energy projects. A US Congressional report published in 2018 reinforced this impression (Congressional Research Service, 2020). The MDBs, it said, "provide financial assistance to developing countries for large infrastructure projects, such as highways, power plants, port facilities, and dams, as well as social projects."

The MDBs also consider themselves to be "major players" in infrastructure. A joint statement issued in 2014 by the World Bank together with half a dozen long-established regional development banks noted pointedly that they "work on the ground in countries at all levels of development to support the full life cycle of infrastructure development" ("Statement", 2014). This piece of collective self-promotion was seen as a response to the challenge from the China-led AIIB. China had at that time also set up the "Silk Road Fund" and had joined other leading emerging economies in establishing the New Development Bank (or BRICS Bank) in Shanghai. These new institutions had announced their intention to focus lending specifically on infrastructure financing rather than getting bogged down with myriad other socio-economic objectives. Their arrival on the scene challenged the more nebulous approach of the existing MDBs.

The rather self-congratulatory tone of the MDBs joint statement in 2014 masked the fact that the aggregate US$130 billion of infrastructure financing which they claimed in their statement to be providing annually at that time pales into insignificance alongside the total current spending on infrastructure and against estimated future needs ("Statement", 2014). This figure was considerably larger than estimates from other sources such as the ODI in London have suggested are being provided directly by the MDBs for infrastructure financing, but the difference appears to be mainly definitional.

In any case, the amounts provided are relatively small compared to actual overall infrastructure spending and to estimated future needs. The Global Infrastructure Hub (formed by the Group of 20 advanced and emerging economies) has estimated that global spending on infrastructure from all sources needs to increase from around US$2.7 trillion annually (as of 2019) to US$3.7 trillion during the period up to 2040, or even higher if this infrastructure is to be protected from climate change.

Thus, while the sums of money provided by MDBs may sound substantial in absolute terms, they are in fact very small relative to the actual spending trend and future needs. They appear modest indeed, for example, when compared to the US$3.7 trillion dollars annual amount (or US$94 trillion in total) that G20 nations, which account for 85 per cent of global GDP, will need to spend every year on average between now and 2040 if the world is to have the infrastructure needed to cope with an estimated population of some US$9 billion people by the end of that time. And it is also small compared to the estimated US$1 trillion a year "financing gap" between what is being spent now from all sources and what is estimated will be required in future in developing nations alone.

In terms of direct contributions to infrastructure financing, the MDBs thus remain relatively small fry. In Asia, for example, the Asian Development Bank has estimated that direct contributions on its own part and by other development banks including by the World Bank currently amount to less than 3% of the total infrastructure funding (Asian Development Bank, 2017). And yet Asia is the world's most populous and fastest-growing region (although that growth is threatened now by infrastructure deficiencies). In Asia, more generally, national governments shoulder by far the biggest share of the burden of financing infrastructure, especially in developing and emerging economies.

Even the total accumulated size of the MDB's infrastructure portfolio, which stood at around US$600 billion as of the end of

2016 according to Britain's Overseas Development Institute, is very small in relation to overall spending on infrastructure (Hart, Miller, & Krause, 2015). The World Bank alone accounts for more than one-half of the portfolio of outstanding loans and regional multilateral banks for slightly more than 30 per cent (see Fig. 12.2).

MDBs, it is true, do "catalyse" quite substantial amounts of private investment into infrastructure simply as a result of "being there" and acting as partners, guarantors, or comfort blankets. As the ODI has put it, "MDBs play an important role as catalysts for private

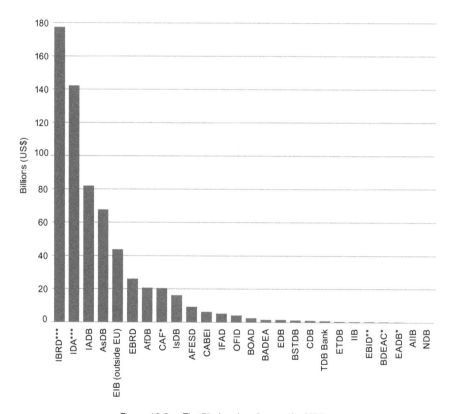

Figure 12.2.   The Big Lenders Among the MDBs.

Source: Prizzon, A. and Engen, L. (2018). *A Guide to Multilateral Development Banks*. London: Overseas Development Institute, p. 30.

investments in various ways (project design, policy advice, co-investor, insurance, etc.). The protective umbrella provided by MDBs is a sign of creditworthiness to private sector investors" (Prizzon & Engen, 2018).

But the amounts involved are again modest in relation to needs. In 2016, for example, the total amount of long-term co-financing mobilised by the dozen leading MDBs (including the World Bank) from insurance companies, pension funds, and sovereign wealth funds and others was US$164 billion (Prizzon & Engen, 2018). Of this, US$69 billion was long-term co-financing for power plants, water, transportation, telecoms, IT, and social infrastructure such as schools and hospitals.

A United Nations International Conference on Financing for Development in 2015 suggested that financial resources needed to achieve the UN Sustainable Development Goals (within which infrastructure is a key element) "far exceed current financial flows" (United Nations, 2015b). It was proclaimed boldly at this meeting that the world needs to "move from billions to trillions of [dollars] of financing in order to meet the challenge of promoting inclusive, sustainable growth, reducing poverty and inequality, and protecting the planet." Yet, where infrastructure is concerned, MDBs deal only in billions of dollars rather than in thousands of billions.

The MDBs are aware of the need to do more. They acknowledged in their 2014 joint statement that infrastructure is key to tackling poverty and promoting inclusive growth. The infrastructure gap in emerging and in developing economies, they said, "is broadly estimated at over US$1 trillion a year." Meeting these needs will require renewed efforts to mobilise resources from existing and new sources of finance. Having made this valid point and while adding that they have the knowledge and experience to leverage greater private involvement in infrastructure worldwide, the MDBs then sidestepped the critical issue of how to boost their own role in this regard. They suggested instead that "the critical barrier to achieving an uplift in infrastructure investment in emerging and developing economies is not a lack of available finance, but an insufficient pipeline of bankable projects ready to be implemented."

There is arguably no more effective way to make infrastructure projects bankable, however, than by involving the MDBs themselves which were purpose-built to tackle the challenges involved. But they have appeared reticent about suggesting this for fear that, by doing so, they might offend their numerous political constituencies by asking for more financial and other resources and that they be allowed to act like banks and not as one-stop agencies for providing a multitude of different socio-economic services. Instead, the MDBs are forced to straighten the way for private investors who are reluctant to enter the infrastructure field unless its bankability is guaranteed and the risk elements all but removed from it. The MDBs have become parties to a charade that has been in vogue since neo-liberal economic views took hold in the US and beyond in the 1980s — that anything the public sector can do, the private sector can do better, and nowhere more so than in the area of infrastructure.

Yet, as was pointed out in a study, private investment tends to be "picky" about where it goes as far as infrastructure is concerned (Yescombe & Farquharson, 2018). There is no denying the fact that private investment has contributed significantly to infrastructure development, "this study observed." However, it has been concentrated in less risky subsectors, reflecting a lower appetite for risk among private investors. This, said Elsevier, "raises questions about how governments can best tap private operators' abilities in high-need and, high-risk area such as water and electricity distribution." Recent projects in these areas indicate that the public sector together with the international financial institutions remains the main source of funding.

In line with this view, a series of "dedicated project preparation facilities" have been launched by the leading MDBs in Europe, the Middle East, Asia, and Africa, as well as in conjunction with the World Bank's Global Infrastructure Facility. These require the MDBs to "work together to develop global public goods and knowledge sharing tools, including standard documentation covering project identification, preparation, procurement, monitoring and supervision, and capacity-building as well as standardised procurement policies" (Yescombe & Farquharson, 2018). These agencies are designed to "provide a global platform for greater collaboration in preparing and structuring complex infrastructure projects" among governments, financial institutions, and private sector partners (L. Jin, personal communication).

Due diligence of infrastructure projects is obviously needed, but assigning such roles to the MDBs when they are not used also as principal providers of finance appears to be a case of giving "responsibility without privilege" (rather than vice versa). It misses the basic but essential point that relegating development banks to the role of advisors when they are constructed to act as financial principals is bordering upon wasteful if not absurd. If MDBs were empowered to exploit fully their fund-raising capability in international capital markets, it might indeed be possible to move from "billions to trillions" of dollars in terms of securing the finance needed for infrastructure, but not otherwise.

In earlier decades, MDBs employed legions of engineering and other specialists to assess the feasibility and supervise the construction of infrastructure projects. Nowadays, they are more likely to employ legions of sociology, medical, and liberal arts graduates to pursue an infinite variety of other tasks at a time when infrastructure-building capacity has never been needed more badly. The China-led AIIB has come closer than any other institution to grasping the necessity to act like a bank rather than merely an advisory body. So far, the AIIB's financing activities have been modest with infrastructure loans of several billions of dollars, but it is building expertise slowly and carefully. As the bank's capability develops, and its activities mesh more closely with those of China's Belt and Road Initiative, it seems likely the AIIB could become an institution on which other MDBs can (re) model themselves.

Economic development is often about competing priorities, and nowhere do these manifest themselves more clearly than in the area of infrastructure. There is the question of whether poverty alleviation should take precedence over infrastructure building, or is infrastructure provision in itself the best way to alleviate poverty? Should developing countries tap foreign capital to finance infrastructure or first develop their own capital markets as a funding source? How can new sources of revenue be tapped to subsidise the cost of infrastructure and increase financial returns to investors? And is it possible to devise new funding models that transform potential future benefits from infrastructure into current revenue streams in order to offset upfront costs?

President and Chairman of the AIIB, Jin Liqun argues for the primacy of infrastructure building. Poverty reduction, he says, has become a mantra for MDBs not least the World Bank and the Asian Development Bank. Yet, so general a concept ought not to be treated as a mission statement and allowed to divert attention from concrete objectives such as infrastructure development. "While poverty reduction is a laudable cause and a poster child for the virtue of development banks it does not go very far in and of itself (L. Jin, personal communication). Broad-based economic and social development is the ultimate solution for poverty reduction."

His words go to the heart of the debate over whether development banks have become so preoccupied with multiple social and economic objectives loosely linked to poverty that they are neglecting their primary function of intermediating finance from international capital markets to finance infrastructure. Jin is not the only one to argue that MDBs have become obsessed with nebulous aims like reducing poverty that they have become unfocussed and ineffective.

"The real experience in much of Asia is that infrastructure construction has had a meaningful impact on improving the lives of ordinary people" says Jin. "There is empirical evidence showing an undeniable link between infrastructure investment and economic growth." He also makes the point that, largely owing to the benefits of improved infrastructure, China has managed to lift over 500 million people out of poverty by World Bank standards, and 600 million by China's standards, in a little over two decades, with the percentage of the population living in poverty falling from 65% in 1981 to just 4 per cent in 2007. "The experience of Asia is that infrastructure construction has had a meaningful impact on improving people's lives," says Jin.

The AIIB which formally opened its doors for business in 2016 was designed specifically as an "infrastructure" bank rather than a broader "development" bank. This reflected a Chinese perception that infrastructure bottlenecks in the world's fastest growing region (Asia) would multiply if development effort and finance continued to be spread so thinly over so wide a range of objectives, Jin acknowledges, that the missions of MDBs vary according to their articles of incorporation. "It is certainly necessary for some MDBs to address poverty reduction directly with their concessional funding. In most cases, however, the approach needs to be refined and improved." There is little point in viewing poverty reduction *per se* as an objective unless this is linked to a specific strategy to improve income and welfare, and the "connectivity" infrastructure provides is a potent means to achieve this end, he suggests.

The types of infrastructure most likely to contribute to growth, Jin suggests, "are those that create jobs, pave the path for private sector development, and generate tax revenues through increased economic activity. If a region lacks transport infrastructure, then roads, railways or ports are what is needed. If it lacks access to clean drinking water, water treatment is the most crucial, power transmission is the most pressing need."

In the debate over how to close the infrastructure financing gap, especially in developing and emerging economies, one factor being overlooked is that liberal savings exist locally, although not in a form where they can easily be channelled into infrastructure. As Asian Development Bank President, Takehiko Nakao sees it, this is a key issue that needs to be addressed. "There are huge savings in many developing countries and how to channel those savings to investment in infrastructure is a very important agenda," the former Vice Finance Minister of Japan argues (personal communication). Instead of relying heavily upon foreign investment and borrowing, governments need to make greater efforts to collect domestic funds.

"One channel can be through government bond issuance and many countries can now issue bonds of investment grade that can be used to finance investment. But countries should also make further efforts to enhance tax revenues. Tax revenues to GDP ratios are often too low. They also should use government borrowing to invest in productive infrastructure." Nakao acknowledges that "schemes to involve domestic and overseas investors in infrastructure development by means of Public-Private Partnership or PPP schemes can make a valuable contribution to huge funding needs, but he cautions against over-reliance on such methods." We should promote PPP although it is a long-term contract between the government and private sector and how to share the risks and costs and set up dispute mechanisms is a challenge. Many countries are paying attention to PPP, partly because they want to build more infrastructure using private sector money as well as fiscal [funds] money and also because they want to draw on the expertise of the private sector for management and technology.

"I think there is a simplistic view that if there is long term money such as pension and life assurance funds, we can simply connect it to a pipeline [of projects]. But it's not so easy." It may be better, Nakao suggests, if portfolio investors buy government bonds structured to suit infrastructure financing because then "they do not need to worry about the government defaulting", whereas investing in individual PPP projects does not allow investors to hedge against risks that arise from changes in government regulation.

His observations cut to the heart of the infrastructure financing dilemma; savings are generally not being collected and channelled into infrastructure in an efficient manner by governments, and neither are capital markets performing this function efficiently. Yet, simply raising taxes or diverting savings from consumption to investment carries the risk of reducing growth in the short term. However, investment in infrastructure can boost economic activity and also employment, thereby augmenting savings and consumption. What this implies is that political courage is needed in the choice of development priorities and the structuring of financial systems so as to emphasise long-term economic growth.

Nakao acknowledges the need for MDBs to play a greater combined role in infrastructure financing and to coordinate their activities in this area (as they have been urged to do by the G20 group of nations). "There is a shortage of money, so the more [institutions involved] the better," he says. The ADB (2017) estimates that developing Asian nations need to invest US$26 trillion between 2016 and 2030 or US$1.7 trillion per year, if the region is to maintain its growth momentum, eradicate poverty, and respond to climate change. Currently, the region annually invests an estimated US$881 billion in infrastructure (for 25 economies with adequate data, comprising 96% of the region's population). The investment gap — the difference between investment needs and current investment levels — equals 2.4 percent of the projected GDP.

Despite the number of players involved now in Asian infrastructure (the ADB itself, the AIIB, the Eurasian Development Bank (EDB), the New Development (BRICS) Bank, the European Bank for Reconstruction and Development and the World Bank, to name just some), Nakao does not worry about potential overlap of efforts among them. "People like to depict the AIIB and the ADB [in particular] as rivals and as competing and uncoordinated organisations but it's not true," says Nakao. "We have been coordinating closely."

Challenges and issues are common, despite the number of players involved in Asian infrastructure (the ADB itself, the AIIB, the EDB, the New Development (BRICS) Bank, the European Bank for Reconstruction and Development and the World Bank to name just some). Nakao does not worry about potential overlap of efforts among them.

"Because of the advent or new players like the AIIB and the New Development Bank we are given an incentive to make our bank even more efficient and better," he says, adding that the ADB had already begun reforms before the idea of the AIIB was floated in late 2013. The ADB has also engineered a major increase in its own lending ability through combining ordinary capital and other funds. The bank began exploring this idea in August 2013 after Nakao became president in that year, and since the ADB made an innovative move, other MDBs have followed suit.

Aside from the push by regional development banks to attack infrastructure deficiencies, Japan has discontinued its bilateral infrastructure initiatives in Asia quite dramatically since Prime Minister

Shinzo Abe announced that Japan would inject additional resources to help develop high-quality Asian infrastructure. This includes a partnership agreement with the ADB to provide US$16 billion over 5 years to support the construction of "sustainable" infrastructure development in Asia and the Pacific while relaxing conditions on providing yen loans for infrastructure in emerging Asian nations. Japan has also boosted the resources of the Japan Bank for International Cooperation (JBIC) and the Japan International Cooperation Agency (JICA) as well as injecting more money into the ADB.

Nakao bridles, however, at any suggestion that the ADB has a special relationship with Japan. "We don't regard just Japan as our partner," he says. "Any partnership or support to the ADB from other countries is welcome and we will seek similar arrangements with other development partners. I don't like the idea that the ADB is regarded as a heavily Japanese-influenced organisation. We have been a truly multilateral Asian institution since the bank was established in 1966. That is our basic spirit."

China's launching of the AIIB has since prompted other leading nations — notably the United States and Canada — to pursue the idea of national infrastructure banks. A plan has been discussed in the US Congress for a government-owned corporation that would provide cheap, long-term financing for infrastructure. Supporters say that this could overcome the fractured nature of local spending, help coordinate developments that cross state borders, and give Washington greater ability to prioritize important projects, as is the case with the European Investment Bank. But so far, the proposal has made little progress. In June 2017, the White House released its 2018 infrastructure budget proposal which built upon US President Donald Trump's election campaign promise of an infrastructure plan worth US$1 trillion ("Fact Sheet", 2017). The proposal relied mainly, however, on private capital that was supposed to be catalysed by US$200 billion of new federal spending, including low-cost loans. But the plan has been criticised as being wholly inadequate to meet the needs of a huge country whose poor infrastructure can impose large costs on the economy and where catastrophic failures such as bridge collapses, dam breaches, inadequately maintained roads, railways, and waterways cost billions of dollars in lost production (not to mention human lives).

Canada did establish a new public institution in 2017, the Canada Infrastructure Bank — a Crown corporation that "operates at arm's length from government and is governed by a Board of Directors." Part of an Investing in Canada plan, the bank is designed to help provincial, territorial, municipal, and "Indigenous partners" build infrastructure across Canada. Again, however, the bank has been heavily criticised, in this case, for over-emphasising the role of private financing at the expense of the public sector.

The failure to make proper use of MDBs is part of a wider failure on the part of policymakers in advanced economies to grasp the full dimensions of the infrastructure gap and what needs to be done in order to close it. Institutional resources do exist to address the problem, but they are not being properly utilised. Likewise, financial resources do exist, but these are not being channelled effectively into infrastructure. It may require an infrastructure crisis in order to drive home the full import of these failures.

CONCLUSION

THE NEED FOR NEW THINKING ON INFRASTRUCTURE

If global economic growth and social welfare are not to suffer in coming years, the problem of how to provide supporting infrastructure in the shape of transport, energy, communications, and other networks must be tackled with much greater vigour and urgency than done at present. Solutions will need to be economically feasible and politically bold as what is required is nothing short of a revolution in perceptions about the importance of infrastructure. A new consensus needs to be forged, in advanced economies especially, on the importance of infrastructure as a key driver of economic growth and as a pillar of social welfare. Achievement of such a consensus would provide the political momentum needed to overcome the many obstacles — ideological and financial — that lie in the path of change and reform.

The vision of infrastructural renewal, with all it implications for higher standards of living, greater prosperity, reduction of poverty, and stronger economic growth and prosperity, needs to be promoted by governments in advanced and developing nations alike. It must be held up before electorates as an exciting and achievable goal in order to secure the needed political consensus. This will, of course, involve ecological challenges if new and greatly extended

149

infrastructure provision across sectors, countries, and continents is not to inflict damage upon the environment. But turning away from such challenges rather than confronting them with the aid of new thinking and new technologies will be as futile as trying to stop the march of time and of progress.

The multiple billions (trillions even) of dollars of investment required to finance the infrastructure revolution will need to come from two basic sources — tax revenues and from savings invested in infrastructure through the mechanism of financial markets. There is a whole new wave of "sustainable investment" waiting to flow into infrastructure and other so-called "alternative" and "sustainable" assets (as has noted earlier in this book). But this requires that conduits for private savings to flow into sustainable investment in infrastructure and other critical areas be more clearly identified. The needed huge sums of money are far more likely to flow freely if savers and electorates are persuaded of the rewards they can expect to reap in the future.

This means that policymakers need to take a much more active interest in infrastructure than is the case at present. It demands that politicians educate themselves better on the rewards of investing in infrastructure and the risks of neglecting such investment and that they in turn make a convincing case to voters for increased spending. It requires legislators in economically advanced nations to become aware of the danger that their countries will be overtaken by emerging nations when it comes to building land and maritime infrastructure networks. Such networks will enable the emerging economies to project strategic and economic power increasingly and to exert "soft power" influence around the world.

The financial community also needs to take a more active and imaginative approach toward funding infrastructure projects and toward "selling" the opportunities that the sector offers to investors.

Banks, securities houses, fund managers, and others must present infrastructure as the preferred longer-term route compared to a narrow focus on short-term consumption and capital gains. Governments and multilateral development banks will need to issue more debt and other financial instruments that are identifiably related to infrastructure, so that institutional and individual investors are able to buy into the infrastructure "revolution". Financial markets too will need to be more imaginative in devising ways to market infrastructure investment via equity, debt and other financial instruments.

The first step is to acknowledge the fact that infrastructure is "special" not just because of the huge financial investments required but also because of the length of time such investments take to yield returns and the difficulty of pricing services at a level where they are affordable yet where they also enable investment to be recovered. In short, infrastructure investment must be "targeted and nurtured". Government balance sheets are big enough to take at least some of the financial strain involved, and only governments can provide regulatory, legal, and other frameworks needed to underpin infrastructure projects. There can be no question of simply "handing the job over" to the private sector. Governments need to stay in the game or even reinforce their role as direct providers of services while also underwriting risks on major projects.

All this may run up against arguments that bureaucracies are inefficient and susceptible to corruption and that the expertise needed to build and operate infrastructure lies chiefly within the private sector. But the fact remains that private sector competencies are not being deployed to anything like the extent needed to "do the job" and the public sector shoulders most of the burden. The quality of public sector effort in infrastructure could be improved through increased funding, enabling more and higher quality management and other talent along with the other resources to be procured by the public sector. This implies increased investment in human and other resources, but the return on investment could be high in terms of improved efficiency.

Efficiency and transparency can be improved by "corporatising" government operations in infrastructure. Corporatisation has been resorted to where governments have used it as a "staging post" en route to privatisation of infrastructure. There is no reason why the principle should not be applied more widely for its own sake rather than as a steppingstone towards privatisation. The reason for maintaining a strong public sector presence is that governments need to be able to perform a "comfort blanket" role in infrastructure (which experience has shown to be essential if private enterprise is to become involved as a partner). This does not prevent governments from utilising the skills of private contractors where needed.

A key question is where the money to finance greater public sector investment in infrastructure and in improving the quality of public governance is to be found. Increased taxes would not be popular and fiscal deficits caused by higher borrowing would not be welcome (although these could be tolerated if it was shown that they were caused by revenue-generating investments). The answer is to shift more public financing of infrastructure "off balance sheet" so far as national accounts are concerned; there are various ways of achieving this (such as, for example, the Japanese government's Fiscal Investment and Loan Programme). Governments must also devise new ways of directing savings into infrastructure through national savings schemes or by launching provident fund-like institutions (the Singapore model) with specific targets.

All this will not be readily accepted in advanced economies where markets nowadays dictate the flow of private savings (and where long-term public investment is often neglected). In these economies, public projects that could serve the economic and social good in the longer term are required to pass "the market test" by proving that they are "bankable." Many fail to do so because the bar is set too high in terms of expected yields on investment, which in turn are dictated by a short-term investment ethos. Market forces are supposed to direct capital to where it is needed and to represent the most efficient way of managing resources. The idea that markets could be short-sighted in preferring short-term gain to long-term economic interest seems to elude many.

Private investors have looked at the risk–reward ratio in infrastructure and decided that it is not for them. Irrespective of the fact that investments in transport, energy, and communications facilities can bring strong financial returns in the longer term, there are "lower-hanging fruits" to be had in the form of myriad investment products and asset classes in capital markets. This is true of most financial institutions, be they banks, pension funds, insurance companies, or private equity funds. Either that or regulations they are required to observe tie their hands when it comes to making investments that pay off only in the long term. The result is a no-man's land where infrastructure goes underfunded as governments wait for the market to shoulder the burden while markets looks to the state to minimise risk.

Is there a way around this dilemma? The answer is yes, provided that politicians and governments in market economies adopt more dirigiste approaches towards infrastructure financing, in contrast to the *laissez-faire* attitudes that have prevailed in recent decades. The concept of "national savings" needs to be revived, whereby governments or their agents collect savings for use in national projects. This has a certain wartime ring to it, but we are, as this book argues, involved in infrastructure wars now. This could supply the "missing link" or channel for directing the private savings of market economies into infrastructure.

National savings can be collected through a variety of means including government-supported provident funds to which employers and employees contribute or from national or municipal bonds dedicated to infrastructure financing. Unlike fiscal channels for financing infrastructure, official savings schemes are obliged to repay providers of funds. The argument here has been that governments in market economies should play a bigger role in infrastructure financing not only by directing more tax revenues into this critical sector but also by guaranteeing infrastructure projects so that institutional investors are willing to buy into them on a much larger scale than is the case at present. This would involve a significant increase in contingent liabilities on the public sector, but because of tax and other revenue streams, governments are equipped to take a longer-term view of risk than are private sector institutions. The returns that infrastructure projects yield over time would justify governments in performing the role of guarantor.

Multilateral development banks such as the World Bank and regional development banks exist basically for the purpose of financing infrastructure. Yet, these institutions provide only around US$130 billion for infrastructure each year compared to the needs running into trillions of dollars. They catalyse billions of dollars of private money in co-financing, but as the Group of 20 advanced and emerging economies has said, these "billions need to become trillions" ("2030 Agenda", n.d.). The MDBs have not been permitted to assume a wider role because the Washington Consensus that guides the policies of many of them dictates that they must not usurp the role of the private sector (even though it is manifestly unable or unwilling to fulfil that role). Instead, they go through a tortuous process of trying to involve private investment in the construction of infrastructure when they could do the job of channelling finance into projects better themselves if only they were allowed to.

Economic development needs to be underpinned by a massive investment in infrastructure, without which growth will stall and welfare will suffer. Some countries such as China have realised this and they seem certain to win the economic development "war" unless others change their thinking and restructure their systems so that they are able to meet the infrastructure challenge. The winners in global infrastructure competition will be those nations that embrace these broader views of economic development while the losers will be those that stick to a narrower vision of infrastructure. The world (advanced nations in particular) has yet to accept that short-term economic growth is being "bought" at the cost of long-term, sustainable development.

BIBLIOGRAPHY

Abe, Xi agree to move from competition to cooperation toward new era in bilateral ties. (2018, October 26). *Shimbun Mainichi*. Retrieved from https://mainichi.jp/english/articles/20181026/p2a/00m/0na/041000c

Anti-corruption and integrity in the public sector. (n.d.). Retrieved from OECD: https://www.oecd.org/gov/ethics/

Asian Development Bank. (2007). *Supporting the fight against Corruption in Asia and the Pacific: The ADB/OECD Anti-Corruption Initiative Annual Report 2008*. Annual Report. Retrieved from http://www.oecd.org/site/adboecdanti-corruptioninitiative/40485068.pdf

Asian Development Bank. (2017). *Meeting Asia's Infrastructure Needs*. Manila: Asian Development Bank. doi:10.22617/FLS168388-2

Basel Institute on Governance. (2016). *Annual Report 2016*. Retrieved from https://www.baselgovernance.org/sites/default/files/2018-12/annual_report_2016.pdf

Blanchard, M.A. (2019, April 29). *Canada's Private Sector Needed to Achieve SDGs*. Retrieved from The Future Economy: https://thefutureeconomy.ca/spotlights/impact-economy/marc-andre-blanchard/

Business Roundtable. (2019, August 19). *Business Roundtable Redefines the Purpose of a Corporation to Promote 'An Economy That Serves All Americans'*. Retrieved from Business Roundtable: https://www.businessroundtable.org/business-roundtable-redefines-the-purpose-of-a-corporation-to-promote-an-economy-that-serves-all-americans

Chavers, K., Synnott, A., Parkes, M., & Pilibossian, A. (2015, November). Infrastructure Investment: Bridging the Gap Between Public and Investor Needs. *Viewpoint*. Retrieved from https://www.blackrock.

com/corporate/literature/whitepaper/viewpoint-infrastructure-investment-november-2015.pdf

Chen, Y., Matzinger, S., & Woetzel, J. (2013, June). Chinese infrastructure: The big picture. *McKinsey Quarterly*. Retrieved from https://www.mckinsey.com/featured-insights/winning-in-emerging-markets/chinese-infrastructure-the-big-picture

Congressional Research Service. (2020). *Multilateral Development Banks: Overview and Issues for Congress* . Retrieved from https://fas.org/sgp/crs/row/R41170.pdf

DeGood, K. (2014). *Public-Private Partnerships: Understanding the Difference Between Procurement and Finance*. Center for American Progress. Retrieved from https://www.americanprogress.org/issues/economy/reports/2014/12/08/102515/public-private-partnerships/

Fact Sheet: 2018 Budget: Infrastructure Initiative. (2017, June). Retrieved from White House: https://www.whitehouse.gov/sites/whitehouse.gov/files/omb/budget/fy2018/fact_sheets/2018%20Budget%20Fact%20Sheet_Infrastructure%20Initiative1.pdf

Fink, L. (2019, January). *Larry Fink's Letter to CEOs*. Retrieved May 5, 2020, from BlackRock: https://www.blackrock.com/corporate/investor-relations/larry-fink-ceo-letter

Fuerer, G. (2015, October 21). *How can we bridge the $1 trillion infrastructure gap?* Retrieved from World Economic Forum: https://www.weforum.org/agenda/2015/10/how-can-we-bridge-the-1-trillion-infrastructure-gap/

G20 Leaders' Communique: Hangzhou Summit. (2016, September). Retrieved from European Council: https://www.consilium.europa.eu/en/meetings/international-summit/2016/09/04-05/

Gemson, J., Gautami, K. V., & Rajan, A. T. (2012, June). Impact of private equity investments in infrastructure projects. *Utilities Policy*, 21, 59–65. doi:https://doi.org/10.1016/j.jup.2011.12.001

George, A., Kaldany, R.-R., & Losavio, J. (2019, April 11). The world is facing a $15 trillion infrastructure gap by 2040. Here's how to bridge it. *World Economic Forum*. Retrieved from https://www.weforum.org/agenda/2019/04/infrastructure-gap-heres-how-to-solve-it/

Global Impact Investing Network. (n.d.). *What You Need to Know about Impact Investing*. Retrieved from Global Impact Investing Network: https://thegiin.org/impact-investing/need-to-know/

Global Infrastructure Hub. (n.d.). Retrieved from Global Infrastructure Hub : https://www.gihub.org/

Government of Canada. (2019, September 30). *Canada's Address to the 74th Session of the United Nations General Assembly, delivered by Ambassador Marc-André Blanchard.* Retrieved from Canada.ca: https://www.international. gc.ca/world-monde/international_relations-relations_internationales/ un-onu/statements-declarations/2019-09-UN-74-NU.aspx?lang=eng

Hart, T., Miller, M., & Krause, P. (2015, November). *Infrastructure development: ambition versus reality.* Retrieved from Overseas Development Institute: https://www.odi.org/opinion/10050-infographics-infrastructure-development-ambition-reality

Hillman, J. E. (2018, April 3). How Big is China's Belt and Road? *Commentary.* Retrieved from https://www.csis.org/analysis/how-big-chinas-belt-and-road

International Finance Corporation. (2019). *Creating Impact: The Promise of Impact Investing.* Washington, D.C.: International Finance Corporation. Retrieved from https://www.ifc.org/wps/wcm/connect/publications_ext_content/ifc_external_publication_site/publications_listing_page/promise-of-impact-investing

International Monetary Fund. (2019). *Global Financial Stability Report: Lower for Longer.* Washington, D.C.: International Monetary Fund. Retrieved from https://www.imf.org/en/Publications/GFSR/Issues/2019/10/ 01/global-financial-stability-report-october-2019

Johnson, S. (2018). *Corruption is costing the global economy $3.6 trillion dollars every year.* World Economic Forum. Retrieved from https://www. weforum.org/agenda/2018/12/the-global-economy-loses-3-6-trillion-to-corruption-cach-year-says-u-n

Little, A. (2020, January). *An Infrastructure Plan for the 21st Century.* Retrieved from Global X: https://www.globalxetfs.com/content/files/200110-Infra-structure_for_21st_Century.pdf

Matthews, P. (2016). *This is why construction is so corrupt.* World Economic Forum. Retrieved from https://www.weforum.org/agenda/2016/02/ why-is-the-construction-industry-so-corrupt-and-what-can-we-do-about-it/

McKinsey Global Institute. (2016). *Bridging Global Infrastructure Gaps.* Retrieved from https://www.mckinsey.com/industries/capital-projects-and-infrastructure/our-insights/bridging-global-infrastructure-gaps

Ministry of Foreign Afairs of Japan. (2015, May 21). *Partnership for Quality Infrastructure: Investment for Asia's Future.* Retrieved from Ministry of Foreign Affairs of Japan: https://www.mofa.go.jp/files/000081298.pdf

Ministry of Foreign Affairs of the People's Republic of China. (2013, September 7). *President Xi Jinping Delivers Important Speech and Proposes to Build a Silk Road Economic Belt with Central Asian Countries.* Retrieved from Ministry of Foreign Affairs of the People's Republic of China:

https://www.fmprc.gov.cn/mfa_eng/topics_665678/xjpfwzysiesgjtfh-shzzfh_665686/t1076334.shtml

Ministry of Foreign Affairs of the People's Republic of China. (2016, September 4). *Xi Jinping Chairs G20 Hangzhou Summit and Delivers an Opening Speech.* Retrieved from Ministry of Foreign Affairs of the People's Republic of China: https://www.fmprc.gov.cn/mfa_eng/zxxx_662805/t1395097.shtml

OECD. (2014). *Private Financing and Government Support to Promote Long-Term Investments in Infrastructure.* Retrieved from https://www.oecd.org/daf/fin/private-pensions/Private-financing-and-government-support-to-promote-LTI-in-infrastructure.pdf

OECD. (2015). *Fostering Investment in Infrastructure: Lessons learned from OECD Investment Policy Reviews.* Retrieved from https://www.oecd.org/daf/inv/investment-policy/Fostering-Investment-in-Infrastructure.pdf

OECD. (2018a). *OECD Business and Finance Outlook 2018.* Paris: OECD Publishing. Retrieved from https://doi.org/10.1787/9789264298828-en

OECD. (2018b). *China's Belt and Road Initiative in the Global Trade, Investment and Finance Landscape.* Retrieved from https://www.oecd.org/finance/Chinas-Belt-and-Road-Initiative-in-the-global-trade-investment-and-finance-landscape.pdf

OECD. (2019, July 3). Japan must urgently address long-standing concerns over foreign bribery enforcement. OECD. Retrieved from https://www.oecd.org/newsroom/japan-must-urgently-address-long-standing-concerns-over-foreign-bribery-enforcement.htm

OECD; International Monetary Fund. (2019). *OECD/IMF Reference Note on the Governance of Quality Infrastructure Investment.* Retrieved from https://www.mof.go.jp/english/international_policy/convention/g20/annex6_5.pdf

Oxford Economics. (2017). *Global Infrastructure Outlook.* Oxford: Oxford Economics Ltd; Global Infrastructure Hub.

Partners Group. (2018). *Corporate Sustainability Report.* Partners Group. Retrieved from https://www.partnersgroup.com/en/sustainability/reports/

Pence, M. (2018, November 16). *Remarks by Vice President Pence at the 2018 APEC CEO Summit.* Retrieved from The White House: https://www.whitehouse.gov/briefings-statements/remarks-vice-president-pence-2018-apec-ceo-summit-port-moresby-papua-new-guinea/

Prizzon, A., & Engen, L. (2018). *A guide to multilateral development banks.* London: Overseas Development Institute.

RIS; ERIA; IDE-JETRO. (2017). *Asia Africa Growth Corridor: Partnership for Sustainable and Innovative Development.* RIS Publication Unit.

Statement by the Heads of the Multilateral Development Banks and the IMF on Infrastructure. (2014, November 13). Retrieved from World Bank: https://www.worldbank.org/en/news/press-release/2014/11/13/ statement-heads-multilateral-development-banks-imf-infrastructure

Strauss, H. (2010). Editor's Introduction. *EIB Papers, 15*(1), 11-15. Retrieved from https://www.eib.org/attachments/efs/eibpapers/eibpapers_ 2010_v15_n01_en.pdf

The 2030 Agenda for Sustainable Development. (n.d.). (Global Solutions Initiative Foundation) Retrieved from G20 Insights: https://www.g20-insights.org/policy_area/g20-support-sustainable-development/

The pandemic is hurting China's Belt and Road Initiative. (2020, June 4). *The Economist.* Retrieved from https://www.economist.com/china/ 2020/06/04/the-pandemic-is-hurting-chinas-belt-and-road-initiative

Tiftik, E., Mahmood, K., & Poljak, J. (2020, January). *Global Debt Monitor: Sustainability Matters.* (S. Gibbs, Ed.) Retrieved from Institute of International Finance: https://www.iif.com/Portals/0/Files/content/ Global%20Debt%20Monitor_January2020_vf.pdf

United Nations. (2015a). *Informal summary on United Nations Summit on Sustainable Development 2015.* Retrieved from Sustainable Development Knowledge Platform: https://sustainabledevelopment.un.org/con-tent/documents/8521Informal%20Summary%20-%20UN%20 Summit%20on%20Sustainable%20Development%202015.pdf

United Nations. (2015b). *Report of the third International Conference on Financing for Development.* New York: United Nations. Retrieved from https://www. undocs.org/A/CONF.227/20

United Nations. (2019). *Roadmap for Financing the 2030 Agenda for Sustainable Development.* Retrieved from https://www.un.org/sustainabledevelopment/ wp-content/uploads/2019/07/UN-SG-Roadmap-Financing-the-SDGs-July-2019.pdf

United Nations Conference on Trade and Development. (2014). *World Investment Report 2014.* New York; Geneva: United Nations. Retrieved from https://unctad.org/en/PublicationsLibrary/wir2014_en.pdf

United Nations Department of Public Information. (2018, September 10). Global Cost of Corruption at Least 5 Per Cent of World Gross Domestic Product, Secretary-General Tells Security Council, Citing World Economic Forum Data. *SC/13493.* Retrieved from https://www.un. org/press/en/2018/sc13493.doc.htm

United Nations Office on Drugs and Crime. (2004). United Nations Convention Against Corruption. New York: United Nations. Retrieved

from https://www.unodc.org/documents/brussels/UN_Convention_
Against_Corruption.pdf

United States Department of Justice. (n.d.). *Foreign Corrupt Practices Act.*
Retrieved from United States Department of Justice: https://www.
justice.gov/criminal-fraud/foreign-corrupt-practices-act

Wells, J. (2015). *Corruption in the construction of public infrastructure: Critical
issues in project preparation.* Bergen: Chr Michelsen Institute.

World Bank. (2018). *Private Investment in Infrastructure in Developing Countries
Showed Signs of Recovery in 2017.* The World Bank Group. Retrieved
from https://www.worldbank.org/en/news/press-release/2018/04/
17/private-investment-in-infrastructure-in-developing-countries-
showed-signs-of-recovery-in-2017

World Economic Forum. (2015a). *Global Competitiveness Report 2015 - 2016.*
Retrieved from http://www3.weforum.org/docs/gcr/2015-2016/
Global_Competitiveness_Report_2015-2016.pdf

World Economic Forum. (2015b). *Infrastructure Investment Policy Blueprint:
Country Performance Assessment.* Retrieved from http://www3.weforum.
org/docs/WEF_Infrastructure_Investment_Policy_Blueprint.pdf

Xi, J. (2016, January 16). *Full text of Chinese President Xi Jinping's address at
AIIB inauguration ceremony.* Retrieved from China Daily: https://www.
chinadaily.com.cn/business/2016-01/16/content_23116718.htm

Yescombe, E. R., & Farquharson, E. (2018). *Public-Private Partnerships for
Infrastructure: Principles of Policy and Finance* (2nd ed.). Oxford: Butterworth-
Heinemann.

Yoshino, N., & Abidhadjaev, U. (2016, May). Impact of Infrastructure
Investment on Tax: Estimating Spillover Effects of the Kyushu High-Speed
Rail Line in Japan on Regional Tax Revenue. *(574).* Asian Development
Bank Institute. Retrieved from https://poseidon01.ssrn.com/delivery.php
?ID=578024126025114002105070030001107105030008032048049017077
0230720650890830180951071000050451181110460190960670900130050
1806500200106105803204612709406811407908609810502007804800203
01010891221120000291210830840930

Yoshino, N., Helble, M., & Abidhadjaev, U. (2018). *Financing Infrastructure
in Asia and the Pacific: Capturing Impacts and New Sources.* Tokyo: Asian
Development Bank Institute.

Yoshino, N., Hossain, M., Hendriyetty, N., & Lakhia, S. (2020). Financing
Infrastructure Investment Through Spillover Tax Revenue Sharing:
Evidence from Some Asian Countries. In M. Hossain (Ed.), *Bangladesh's
Economic Policy* (pp. 217-238). Singapore: Palgrave Macmillan.

INDEX

CPSIA information can be obtained
at www.ICGtesting.com
Printed in the USA
BVHW040831170820
585247BV00018B/18